CCSP

CERTIFIED CLOUD SECURITY PROFESSIONAL

NOVICE TO CERTIFIED

4 BOOKS IN 1

BOOK 1
FOUNDATIONS OF CLOUD SECURITY: A BEGINNER'S GUIDE TO CCSP

BOOK 2
SECURING CLOUD INFRASTRUCTURE: ADVANCED TECHNIQUES FOR CCSP

BOOK 3
RISK MANAGEMENT IN THE CLOUD: STRATEGIES FOR CCSP PROFESSIONALS

BOOK 4
MASTERING CLOUD SECURITY: EXPERT INSIGHTS AND BEST PRACTICES FOR CCSP CERTIFICATION

ROB BOTWRIGHT

Published by Rob Botwright
Library of Congress Cataloging-in-Publication Data
ISBN 978-1-83938-782-1
Cover design by Rizzo

Disclaimer

The contents of this book are based on extensive research and the best available historical sources. However, the author and publisher make no claims, promises, or guarantees about the accuracy, completeness, or adequacy of the information contained herein. The information in this book is provided on an "as is" basis, and the author and publisher disclaim any and all liability for any errors, omissions, or inaccuracies in the information or for any actions taken in reliance on such information. The opinions and views expressed in this book are those of the author and do not necessarily reflect the official policy or position of any organization or individual mentioned in this book. Any reference to specific people, places, or events is intended only to provide historical context and is not intended to defame or malign any group, individual, or entity. The information in this book is intended for educational and entertainment purposes only. It is not intended to be a substitute for professional advice or judgment. Readers are encouraged to conduct their own research and to seek professional advice where appropriate. Every effort has been made to obtain necessary permissions and acknowledgments for all images and other copyrighted material used in this book. Any errors or omissions in this regard are unintentional, and the author and publisher will correct them in future editions.

BOOK 1 - FOUNDATIONS OF CLOUD SECURITY: A BEGINNER'S GUIDE TO CCSP

BOOK 2 - SECURING CLOUD INFRASTRUCTURE: ADVANCED TECHNIQUES FOR CCSP

BOOK 3 - RISK MANAGEMENT IN THE CLOUD: STRATEGIES FOR CCSP PROFESSIONALS

BOOK 4 - MASTERING CLOUD SECURITY: EXPERT INSIGHTS AND BEST PRACTICES FOR CCSP CERTIFICATION

BOOK 1
FOUNDATIONS OF CLOUD SECURITY
A BEGINNER'S GUIDE TO CCSP

ROB BOTWRIGHT

Introduction

Welcome to the "CCSP: Certified Cloud Security Professional - Novice to Certified" book bundle, a comprehensive resource designed to guide you on your journey to becoming a proficient and certified cloud security professional. In today's rapidly evolving digital landscape, cloud computing has become the backbone of modern business operations, offering unparalleled flexibility, scalability, and efficiency. However, with the benefits of cloud adoption come unique security challenges that require specialized knowledge and expertise to address effectively.

This book bundle consists of four distinct volumes, each meticulously crafted to provide a structured pathway from novice to certified cloud security professional. Whether you are new to the field or seeking to enhance your existing skills, this bundle covers everything you need to know to succeed in the dynamic and complex world of cloud security.

Book 1 - Foundations of Cloud Security: A Beginner's Guide to CCSP: In this foundational volume, readers are introduced to the fundamental concepts, principles, and components of cloud security. From understanding the shared responsibility model to exploring essential security controls and best practices, this book serves as a comprehensive primer for beginners entering the field of cloud security.

Book 2 - Securing Cloud Infrastructure: Advanced Techniques for CCSP: Building upon the foundational knowledge acquired in Book 1, this volume delves into advanced techniques and strategies for securing cloud infrastructure. From securing multi-cloud environments to implementing advanced encryption and access controls, readers will gain the expertise needed to tackle complex security challenges in modern cloud environments.

Book 3 - Risk Management in the Cloud: Strategies for CCSP Professionals: Risk management is a critical aspect of cloud security, and this volume explores the principles and strategies tailored specifically for cloud environments. Readers will learn how to identify, assess, and mitigate risks effectively, ensuring the security and resilience of cloud-based systems and applications.

Book 4 - Mastering Cloud Security: Expert Insights and Best Practices for CCSP Certification: In the final volume of this book bundle, readers will gain access to expert insights and best practices from seasoned professionals in the field. This book goes beyond theoretical concepts to provide practical guidance and real-world examples, enabling readers to apply their knowledge effectively and achieve CCSP certification with confidence.

Together, these four volumes form a comprehensive and cohesive resource that empowers readers to become proficient in cloud security and excel in their careers as Certified Cloud Security Professionals. Whether you are just starting your journey or seeking to advance your expertise, this book bundle equips you with the knowledge, skills, and confidence needed to succeed in today's dynamic and ever-evolving cloud landscape.

Chapter 1: Understanding Cloud Computing

Cloud service models, often referred to as Infrastructure as a Service (IaaS), Platform as a Service (PaaS), and Software as a Service (SaaS), represent different layers of cloud computing that offer varying degrees of control, management, and customization to users. IaaS provides virtualized computing resources over the internet, allowing users to rent servers, storage, and networking infrastructure on-demand, typically managed through a web-based dashboard or through APIs. Popular IaaS providers include Amazon Web Services (AWS), Microsoft Azure, and Google Cloud Platform (GCP). With IaaS, users have full control over the operating system, applications, and runtime environment, enabling them to deploy and manage virtual machines, containers, and storage resources according to their specific requirements. For example, deploying a virtual machine on AWS involves using the EC2 (Elastic Compute Cloud) service through the AWS Management Console or via CLI commands like aws ec2 run-instances. PaaS, on the other hand, abstracts away the underlying infrastructure and provides a platform for developers to build, deploy, and manage applications without worrying about the underlying hardware or software stack. PaaS offerings typically include development frameworks, runtime environments, databases, and middleware, allowing developers to focus solely on writing and deploying code. Platforms like Heroku, Microsoft Azure App Service, and Google App Engine exemplify PaaS offerings, where developers can deploy applications written in various programming languages such as Python, Java, or Node.js with minimal setup and configuration. For instance, deploying a web application to Heroku involves pushing code to a Git repository and using the Heroku CLI command heroku create to create a new application instance. SaaS represents the highest level of abstraction in cloud computing, delivering fully functional applications over the internet on a subscription basis. SaaS applications are accessible via web browsers or APIs, eliminating the need for users to install, maintain, or manage any software locally. Examples of SaaS offerings include Google Workspace (formerly G Suite), Microsoft Office 365, and Salesforce. These applications provide a range of productivity tools, collaboration suites, and customer relationship management (CRM) solutions that cater to businesses of all sizes. Deploying a SaaS application typically involves signing up for a subscription plan and configuring user accounts and permissions through an administrative dashboard. Each cloud service model offers distinct advantages and trade-offs in terms of scalability, flexibility, and management overhead. Organizations often leverage a combination of these models, known as cloud deployment models, to meet

their specific business needs. Hybrid cloud, for example, combines public cloud services with on-premises infrastructure, allowing organizations to benefit from the scalability and agility of the cloud while maintaining control over sensitive data and compliance requirements. Multi-cloud takes this a step further by using multiple public cloud providers to avoid vendor lock-in, mitigate risks of service outages, and optimize costs based on workload requirements. Managing cloud service models effectively requires a solid understanding of cloud computing principles, security best practices, and governance frameworks. It's essential for organizations to assess their requirements, evaluate different service models and providers, and develop a comprehensive cloud strategy that aligns with their business objectives. Moreover, continuous monitoring, optimization, and automation are critical for ensuring cost-effectiveness, performance, and compliance across cloud environments. As the cloud computing landscape continues to evolve, with advancements in technologies like serverless computing, edge computing, and artificial intelligence, organizations must remain agile and adaptable to harness the full potential of cloud service models for driving innovation and growth.
Cloud deployment models, such as public cloud, private cloud, hybrid cloud, and multi-cloud, offer organizations various options for deploying and managing their IT infrastructure and applications in

the cloud. Public cloud deployment involves utilizing cloud resources and services provided by third-party cloud service providers, such as Amazon Web Services (AWS), Microsoft Azure, or Google Cloud Platform (GCP), over the internet. Deploying an application on a public cloud typically involves provisioning virtual machines, storage, and other resources through a cloud provider's web-based console or using command-line interface (CLI) commands like aws ec2 run-instances for AWS or gcloud compute instances create for Google Cloud. Public cloud services offer scalability, flexibility, and cost-effectiveness, making them ideal for startups, small businesses, and enterprises alike. Private cloud deployment, on the other hand, involves hosting cloud infrastructure and services within an organization's own data center or on dedicated hardware, providing greater control, security, and compliance compared to public cloud environments. Deploying a private cloud requires configuring and managing virtualization technologies like VMware vSphere or Microsoft Hyper-V, as well as implementing cloud management platforms such as OpenStack or VMware vRealize Suite. Private clouds are often used by industries with strict regulatory requirements, such as finance, healthcare, and government, where data privacy and control are paramount. Hybrid cloud deployment combines elements of both public and private clouds, allowing organizations to leverage the scalability and cost-effectiveness of the public cloud for non-sensitive workloads while keeping critical data and applications on-premises or in a private cloud for enhanced security and compliance. Deploying a hybrid cloud involves integrating on-premises infrastructure with public cloud services using technologies like virtual private networks (VPNs), direct connections, or hybrid cloud management platforms such as AWS Outposts or Azure Arc. Hybrid clouds offer the flexibility to scale resources dynamically based on workload demand while maintaining control over sensitive data and applications. Multi-cloud deployment extends the hybrid cloud model by leveraging multiple public cloud providers simultaneously to avoid vendor lock-in, optimize costs, and enhance redundancy and resilience. Deploying a multi-cloud architecture involves distributing workloads across different cloud providers based on performance, geographic location, or service capabilities, and managing them centrally through cloud management platforms or orchestration tools like Kubernetes. Multi-cloud environments offer organizations the flexibility to choose the best-of-breed services from different cloud providers, mitigate risks of service outages or disruptions, and optimize costs based on workload requirements. However, managing and securing multi-cloud deployments can be complex and challenging, requiring robust governance, automation, and monitoring capabilities. Regardless of the chosen deployment model, organizations must consider factors such as scalability, performance, security, compliance, and cost when designing and implementing their cloud infrastructure and applications. Moreover, ongoing management, optimization, and governance are essential for ensuring the success and effectiveness of cloud deployments in meeting business objectives and driving innovation and growth. As cloud technologies continue to evolve and mature, organizations must stay agile and adaptable to capitalize on emerging trends and opportunities in the ever-changing landscape of cloud computing.

Cloud security challenges encompass a wide range of issues and concerns that organizations face when migrating their data, applications, and infrastructure to the cloud. One of the primary challenges is data security, as organizations must ensure the confidentiality, integrity, and availability of their sensitive data stored in the cloud. Encrypting data at rest and in transit using strong encryption algorithms and implementing access controls and encryption key management practices can help mitigate the risk of data breaches and unauthorized access. However, managing encryption keys securely and ensuring compliance with data privacy regulations such as GDPR (General Data Protection Regulation) or HIPAA (Health Insurance Portability and Accountability Act) can be complex and challenging. Another significant challenge is identity and access management (IAM), as organizations need to authenticate and authorize users, devices, and applications accessing cloud resources. Implementing strong authentication mechanisms such as multi-factor authentication (MFA), role-based access control (RBAC), and least privilege principles can help mitigate the risk of unauthorized access and insider threats. However, managing user identities and permissions across multiple cloud environments and integrating with

14

existing identity systems can be cumbersome and prone to misconfigurations. Additionally, securing cloud infrastructure and services against cyber threats and vulnerabilities is a critical challenge for organizations. Implementing security best practices such as network segmentation, firewalls, intrusion detection and prevention systems (IDS/IPS), and regular vulnerability scanning and patch management can help protect against common threats like malware, DDoS (Distributed Denial of Service) attacks, and data exfiltration. However, ensuring the security of cloud-native services and serverless computing environments requires specialized knowledge and tools for configuration management, monitoring, and incident response. Compliance and regulatory requirements pose another significant challenge for organizations operating in the cloud, as they need to ensure adherence to industry standards and government regulations governing data privacy, security, and residency. Conducting regular compliance audits, implementing security controls and logging mechanisms, and documenting security policies and procedures can help demonstrate compliance with regulations such as PCI DSS (Payment Card Industry Data Security Standard) or SOC 2 (Service Organization Control 2). However, interpreting complex regulatory requirements and ensuring consistency across different cloud environments and regions can be daunting tasks for organizations with diverse business operations and regulatory obligations. Cloud security challenges are further exacerbated by the evolving threat landscape and sophisticated cyber attacks targeting cloud infrastructure and services. Implementing proactive security measures such as threat intelligence, security analytics, and incident response planning can help organizations detect and respond to security incidents effectively. However, keeping pace with emerging threats, vulnerabilities, and attack vectors requires continuous monitoring, threat hunting, and collaboration with industry peers and security experts. Moreover, ensuring the security of third-party cloud services and supply chain partners presents additional challenges, as organizations need to assess the security posture and reliability of cloud providers and vendors. Conducting due diligence, performing security assessments, and establishing contractual agreements and service level agreements (SLAs) can help mitigate the risk of security breaches and service disruptions. However, maintaining oversight and accountability over third-party relationships and dependencies requires ongoing risk management and vendor management practices. In summary, addressing cloud security challenges requires a holistic and proactive approach that encompasses people, processes, and technologies. By adopting a risk-based approach, leveraging security best practices, and collaborating with trusted partners and industry peers, organizations can effectively mitigate the risks associated with cloud computing and harness its benefits for innovation and growth.

The Shared Responsibility Model is a fundamental concept in cloud computing that defines the division of security responsibilities between cloud service providers (CSPs) and their customers. Under this model, CSPs are responsible for securing the underlying infrastructure and services that support the cloud environment, while customers are responsible for securing the data, applications, and configurations they deploy on the cloud platform. This shared responsibility helps clarify roles and obligations, ensuring a more secure cloud computing environment for both parties. In practice, the specifics of the shared responsibility model may vary depending on the type of cloud service being used: Infrastructure as a Service (IaaS), Platform as a Service (PaaS), or Software as a Service (SaaS). In an IaaS environment, CSPs are responsible for securing the physical data centers, networking infrastructure, and hypervisors that host virtual machines and storage resources. Customers, on the other hand, are responsible for securing the operating systems, applications, and data stored within their virtual machines and containers. For example, in Amazon Web Services (AWS), AWS is responsible for the security of the underlying infrastructure, including the physical security of data centers, while customers are responsible for securing their data, applications, and access credentials. This includes implementing security groups, configuring firewalls, and encrypting data at rest and in transit using AWS services such as Amazon EC2 and Amazon S3. In a PaaS environment, CSPs provide a platform for customers to develop, deploy, and manage applications without worrying about the underlying infrastructure. CSPs are responsible for securing the runtime environment, middleware, and development tools provided as part of the platform. Customers, however, are responsible for securing their applications, data, and access controls within the platform. For instance, in Microsoft Azure App Service, Microsoft is responsible for securing the underlying platform infrastructure, including the web servers and databases, while customers are responsible for securing their web applications and databases, implementing role-based access control (RBAC), and configuring network security groups (NSGs). In a SaaS environment, CSPs deliver fully functional applications over the internet on a subscription basis, relieving customers of the burden of managing the underlying infrastructure or application code. CSPs are responsible for securing the application, data, and access controls within the SaaS platform. Customers, however, are responsible for configuring user access, managing data privacy settings, and ensuring compliance with industry regulations. For example, in Salesforce, Salesforce is responsible for securing the Salesforce application and data stored within it, while customers are responsible for configuring user permissions, setting up data encryption, and managing compliance with regulations such as GDPR. In summary, the Shared Responsibility Model is a critical component of cloud security, outlining the respective roles and responsibilities of CSPs and customers in securing the cloud environment. By understanding and adhering to this model, organizations can effectively mitigate security risks and ensure the confidentiality, integrity, and availability of their data and applications in the cloud.

Data encryption techniques play a crucial role in safeguarding sensitive information from unauthorized access and interception, both at rest and in transit, in various computing environments, including on-premises servers, cloud platforms, and mobile devices. Encryption is the process of converting plaintext data into ciphertext using cryptographic algorithms and keys, making it unreadable to anyone without the corresponding decryption key. One of the most commonly used encryption techniques is symmetric encryption, where the same key is used for both encryption and decryption. The encryption and decryption process in symmetric encryption algorithms such as Advanced Encryption Standard (AES) is typically fast and efficient, making it suitable for encrypting large volumes of data. To encrypt data using AES in a command-line interface, one can use the OpenSSL command openssl enc -aes-256-cbc -in plaintext.txt -out encrypted.txt, where -aes-256-cbc specifies the AES encryption algorithm with a 256-bit key in Cipher Block Chaining (CBC) mode, -in plaintext.txt specifies the input plaintext file, and -out encrypted.txt specifies the output encrypted file. However, the main challenge with symmetric encryption is securely sharing the encryption key between the sender and recipient without interception or compromise. Asymmetric encryption, also known as public-key encryption, addresses this challenge by using a pair of keys: a public key for encryption and a private key for decryption. The public key can be freely distributed to anyone, while the private key is kept secret and known only to the intended recipient. To encrypt data using asymmetric encryption in a command-line interface, one can use the OpenSSL command openssl rsautl -encrypt -pubin -in plaintext.txt -inkey public.key -out encrypted.txt, where -encrypt specifies the encryption operation, -pubin specifies that the public key is provided as input, -in plaintext.txt specifies the input plaintext file, -inkey public.key specifies the public key file, and -out encrypted.txt specifies the output encrypted file. Asymmetric encryption ensures secure communication between parties without the need for a pre-shared secret key, making it suitable for secure key exchange and digital signatures. However, asymmetric encryption algorithms are generally slower and computationally intensive compared to symmetric encryption algorithms, making them less suitable for encrypting large volumes of data. Another important aspect of data encryption is key management, which involves securely generating, storing, distributing, and revoking encryption keys to prevent unauthorized access or misuse. Key management practices include key generation using cryptographically secure random number generators, key storage in secure hardware modules or key management systems, key distribution using secure channels or protocols, and key rotation and revocation to mitigate the risk of key compromise. Organizations can also leverage key management services provided by cloud providers such as AWS Key Management Service (KMS) or Azure Key Vault to simplify key lifecycle management and ensure compliance with security best practices. Additionally, data encryption can be enhanced with additional security measures such as data masking, tokenization, and homomorphic encryption to further protect sensitive information and preserve privacy. Data masking involves replacing sensitive data with fictitious or obfuscated values to prevent unauthorized access or exposure. Tokenization replaces sensitive data with randomly generated tokens or placeholders, which can be securely stored and processed without revealing the original data. Homomorphic encryption allows computations to be performed on encrypted data without decrypting it first, preserving the confidentiality of the data throughout the computation process. However, homomorphic encryption is still an emerging technology with practical limitations in terms of performance and scalability. In summary, data encryption techniques are essential for protecting sensitive information and ensuring data confidentiality, integrity, and availability in various computing environments. By implementing strong encryption algorithms, secure key management practices, and additional security measures such as data masking and tokenization, organizations can mitigate the risk of data breaches and unauthorized access, comply with regulatory requirements, and build trust with customers and stakeholders. Data integrity mechanisms are essential components of information security that ensure the accuracy, consistency, and reliability of data throughout its lifecycle, protecting against unauthorized modifications, deletions, or corruption. These mechanisms employ various cryptographic techniques, error detection codes, and validation algorithms to verify the integrity of data and detect any unauthorized changes or tampering attempts. One common method for ensuring data integrity is through the use of cryptographic hash functions, which generate fixed-length hash values or checksums for input data, such as files or messages, in a way that any change to the data will result in a different hash value. A widely used cryptographic hash function is the Secure Hash Algorithm (SHA), which comes in different variants such as SHA-256 or SHA-512, offering different levels of security and collision resistance. To calculate the SHA-256 hash value of a file in a command-line interface, one can use the OpenSSL command openssl dgst -sha256 file.txt, where -sha256 specifies the SHA-256 hash function and file.txt specifies the input file. The resulting hash value can then be compared against a previously computed hash value to verify the integrity of the file.

Another method for ensuring data integrity is through the use of digital signatures, which provide a means of authenticating the origin and integrity of digital documents or messages. Digital signatures are created using asymmetric encryption algorithms and involve the generation of a cryptographic hash value of the data to be signed, followed by the encryption of the hash value using the signer's private key. To create a digital signature for a file in a command-line interface using the OpenSSL command openssl dgst -sha256 -sign private.key -out signature.sha256 file.txt, where -sha256 specifies the SHA-256 hash function, -sign private.key specifies the private key used for signing, and file.txt specifies the input file. The resulting signature can then be verified using the corresponding public key to ensure the integrity and authenticity of the file. Error detection codes, such as cyclic redundancy checks (CRCs) or checksums, are also commonly used for ensuring data integrity, particularly in storage and transmission systems where errors may occur due to noise, interference, or hardware malfunctions. These codes add redundant bits to the data stream, allowing the receiver to detect and correct errors that may have occurred during transmission or storage. To generate a CRC checksum for a file in a command-line interface, one can use the cksum command followed by the file name, which will output the CRC checksum along with the number of bytes in the file. For example, cksum file.txt. Similarly, checksums can be computed using utilities like md5sum, sha1sum, or sha256sum, depending on the desired hash function. In addition to cryptographic hash functions, digital signatures, and error detection codes, data integrity mechanisms may also include measures such as access controls, version control systems, and audit trails, which help prevent unauthorized modifications to data and track changes over time. Access controls restrict access to data based on user permissions and privileges, ensuring that only authorized users can modify or delete data. Version control systems, such as Git or Subversion, maintain a history of changes to files and documents, allowing users to revert to previous versions if necessary and track who made each change. Audit trails record and monitor user activities and system events, providing a means of detecting and investigating unauthorized or suspicious activities that may impact data integrity. By implementing robust data integrity mechanisms, organizations can protect against data tampering, corruption, or loss, ensuring the trustworthiness and reliability of their data assets. These mechanisms play a critical role in maintaining data integrity and ensuring compliance with regulatory requirements, industry standards, and organizational policies. Moreover, data integrity mechanisms help build confidence and trust among stakeholders, customers, and partners, strengthening the organization's reputation and competitiveness in the marketplace.

Secure configuration management is a fundamental aspect of cybersecurity that involves establishing and maintaining secure configurations for hardware, software, and network devices to mitigate security risks and vulnerabilities. It encompasses a range of practices, policies, and procedures aimed at ensuring that systems are configured securely, following industry best practices, security standards, and regulatory requirements. One key aspect of secure configuration management is the hardening of systems, which involves reducing the attack surface and minimizing potential security vulnerabilities by disabling unnecessary services, removing default accounts and passwords, and applying security patches and updates in a timely manner. To harden a Linux system, one can use tools like OpenSCAP or Security Enhanced Linux (SELinux) to perform security scans and audits, identify vulnerabilities, and enforce security policies based on predefined security benchmarks such as CIS (Center for Internet Security) benchmarks. Another important aspect of secure configuration management is the implementation of access controls and least privilege principles to limit user access and permissions to only those necessary for their role or function. This involves configuring user accounts, groups, and permissions on operating systems, databases, and applications to ensure that users have access to only the resources and data they need to perform their job responsibilities. In a command-line interface, one can use utilities like chmod, chown, or setfacl to modify file and directory permissions and useradd, usermod, or userdel to manage user accounts and groups. Additionally, organizations can leverage centralized identity and access management (IAM) solutions such as Microsoft Active Directory or LDAP (Lightweight Directory Access Protocol) directories to streamline user authentication and authorization processes and enforce consistent access controls across multiple systems and applications. Configuration baselines and standards are also essential components of secure configuration management, providing a set of predefined configuration settings and security controls that serve as a baseline for securely configuring systems and devices. Organizations can develop their configuration baselines based on security frameworks such as NIST (National Institute of Standards and Technology) Special Publication 800-53 or industry-specific standards such as PCI DSS (Payment Card Industry Data Security Standard) or HIPAA (Health Insurance Portability and Accountability Act). To enforce configuration baselines, organizations can use configuration management tools like Ansible, Puppet, or Chef to automate the deployment and enforcement of configuration settings across distributed IT environments. These tools allow organizations to define configuration policies as code, track changes, and ensure consistency and compliance with security standards and best practices. Vulnerability management is another critical aspect of secure configuration management, involving the identification, assessment, prioritization, and remediation of security vulnerabilities in systems and software. Organizations can use vulnerability scanning tools like Nessus, Qualys, or OpenVAS to scan for known vulnerabilities and misconfigurations in network devices, servers, and applications, and prioritize remediation efforts based on risk severity and business impact. To remediate vulnerabilities, organizations can apply security patches and updates provided by software vendors or implement compensating controls to mitigate the risk until patches are available or feasible to apply. Additionally, organizations can implement network segmentation and isolation to minimize the impact of security breaches and limit lateral movement within their IT infrastructure. This involves dividing networks into separate segments or zones based on security requirements and applying access controls and firewall rules to restrict communication between segments and enforce the principle of least privilege. By implementing secure configuration management practices, organizations can reduce the likelihood and impact of security incidents, protect sensitive data and critical assets, and maintain compliance with regulatory requirements and industry standards.

These practices help establish a strong security posture, build resilience against cyber threats, and instill confidence and trust among customers, partners, and stakeholders. Moreover, secure configuration management is an ongoing process that requires continuous monitoring, assessment, and improvement to address evolving security threats and vulnerabilities and adapt to changes in technology, business requirements, and regulatory landscapes. Role-Based Access Control (RBAC) is a widely used access control mechanism in information security that restricts system access to authorized users based on their roles and responsibilities within an organization. RBAC assigns permissions to roles rather than individual users, simplifying access management and ensuring consistent enforcement of security policies across the organization. One key component of RBAC is the definition of roles, which represent sets of permissions or privileges associated with specific job functions or responsibilities. These roles are typically defined based on organizational hierarchy, job functions, or business processes and are assigned appropriate permissions to perform their respective tasks. To define roles in RBAC, organizations can use administrative tools or access control management platforms to create role definitions and assign permissions to each role. For example, in a Linux environment, roles can be defined using the roleadd command followed by the name of the role, such as roleadd -r role_name. Once roles have been defined, the next step in RBAC implementation is role assignment, which involves assigning roles to individual users or groups based on their job roles or responsibilities. This allows users to inherit permissions associated with their assigned roles, simplifying access management and reducing the risk of unauthorized access. In a command-line interface, role assignment can be performed using the usermod command followed by the -aG option to add a user to a specific group, such as usermod -aG role_group username. Additionally, organizations can use access control lists (ACLs) or group policies to enforce role assignments and ensure that users are granted appropriate permissions based on their roles. RBAC also includes mechanisms for role authorization, which determine whether a user is allowed to perform a specific action or access a particular resource based on their assigned role and associated permissions. Authorization decisions are typically made by the system based on predefined access control policies or rules that specify which roles are permitted to perform certain actions or access certain resources. In a Linux environment, authorization policies can be defined using tools like sudo or selinux to specify which roles are allowed to execute specific commands or access certain files or directories. RBAC implementation also involves ongoing administration and maintenance activities, such as role review and role adjustment, to ensure that roles remain aligned with organizational requirements and user responsibilities. This includes periodically reviewing role assignments and permissions to identify any discrepancies or unauthorized access and making adjustments as needed to maintain the principle of least privilege. To review role assignments in a Linux environment, organizations can use the getent command followed by the group option to display group membership information, such as getent group role_group. Additionally, organizations should regularly audit access logs and monitor user activity to detect and investigate any suspicious or unauthorized access attempts that may indicate a security breach. RBAC provides several benefits for organizations, including improved security, simplified access management, and enhanced compliance with regulatory requirements. By assigning permissions based on job roles rather than individual users, RBAC helps organizations enforce the principle of least privilege, reducing the risk of unauthorized access and potential security breaches. RBAC also simplifies access management by allowing administrators to manage permissions at the role level rather than for each individual user, streamlining administrative tasks and reducing the potential for errors. Additionally, RBAC supports compliance efforts by providing a structured framework for access control that aligns with regulatory requirements and industry best practices. Overall, RBAC is a powerful access control mechanism that helps organizations improve security, streamline access management, and maintain compliance with regulatory requirements. By implementing RBAC effectively, organizations can reduce the risk of unauthorized access, protect sensitive information, and ensure the confidentiality, integrity, and availability of their IT resources.

Role-Based Access Control (RBAC) is a widely adopted access control mechanism in the field of cybersecurity, providing a structured approach to managing user permissions within an organization's information systems. RBAC restricts system access based on the roles individuals hold within the organization, rather than their individual identities, simplifying the administration of user access rights and ensuring consistent enforcement of security policies. The core concept of RBAC revolves around defining roles, which represent sets of permissions or privileges associated with specific job functions or responsibilities. These roles are defined based on organizational hierarchies, job roles, or business processes, and each role is assigned a distinct set of permissions that dictate what actions users assigned to that role can perform within the system. To define roles in RBAC, organizations typically use administrative tools or access control management platforms to create role definitions and assign corresponding permissions. For example, in a Linux environment, roles can be defined using the roleadd command, specifying the name of the role to be created. Once roles have been defined, the next step in RBAC implementation is role assignment, which involves assigning roles to individual users or groups based on their job responsibilities. This allows users to inherit permissions associated with their assigned roles, ensuring that they have access only to the resources and functionality necessary to perform their duties. In a Linux environment, role assignment can be achieved using the usermod command, followed by the -aG option to add a user to a specific group corresponding to their assigned role. Additionally, organizations can use access control lists (ACLs) or group policies to enforce role assignments and ensure that users are granted appropriate permissions based on their roles. RBAC also includes mechanisms for role authorization, which determine whether a user is allowed to perform a specific action or access a particular resource based on their assigned role and associated permissions. Authorization decisions are typically made by the system based on predefined access control policies or rules that specify which roles are permitted to perform certain actions or access certain resources. In a Linux environment, authorization policies can be defined using tools like sudo or selinux, specifying which roles are allowed to execute specific commands or access certain files or directories. RBAC implementation also involves ongoing administration and maintenance activities, such as role review and adjustment, to ensure that roles remain aligned with organizational requirements and user responsibilities. This includes periodically reviewing role assignments and permissions to identify any discrepancies or unauthorized access and making adjustments as needed to maintain the principle of least privilege. To review role assignments in a Linux environment, organizations can use the getent command, followed by the group option to display group membership information, providing insights into which users are assigned to specific roles. Additionally, organizations should regularly audit access logs and monitor user activity to detect and investigate any suspicious or unauthorized access attempts that may indicate a security breach. RBAC provides several benefits for organizations, including improved security, simplified access management, and enhanced compliance with regulatory requirements. By assigning permissions based on job roles rather than individual users, RBAC helps organizations enforce the principle of least privilege, reducing the risk of unauthorized access and potential security breaches. RBAC also simplifies access management by allowing administrators to manage permissions at the role level rather than for each individual user, streamlining administrative tasks and reducing the potential for errors. Additionally, RBAC supports compliance efforts by providing a structured framework for access control that aligns with regulatory requirements and industry best practices. Overall, RBAC is a powerful access control mechanism that helps organizations improve security, streamline access management, and maintain compliance with regulatory requirements. By implementing RBAC effectively, organizations can reduce the risk of unauthorized access, protect sensitive information, and ensure the confidentiality, integrity, and availability of their IT resources. Multi-Factor Authentication (MFA) is a robust security mechanism that requires users to provide multiple forms of identification before granting access to a system, application, or network, adding an extra layer of protection beyond traditional password-based authentication methods. MFA strengthens security by requiring users to provide two or more authentication factors from different categories, typically something they know (such as a password), something they have (such as a mobile device or security token), or something they are (such as biometric data like fingerprints or facial recognition). One common implementation of MFA involves the use of one-time passwords (OTPs) generated by mobile authenticator apps or hardware tokens, which users must enter along with their regular password to authenticate. To set up MFA using a mobile authenticator app, users typically need to scan a QR code provided by the service or application they are trying to access, which adds the account to the authenticator app and generates OTPs that expire after a short period, enhancing security by requiring users to provide a temporary code in addition to their password when logging in. Another form of MFA is biometric authentication, which relies on unique physical characteristics or behavioral traits of an individual, such as fingerprints, iris scans, or voice recognition, to *verify their identity. Biometric authentication systems capture biometric data from users and compare it against stored templates to determine if a match exists, providing an additional layer of security by verifying users based on who they are rather than what they know or have. To implement biometric authentication, organizations can deploy biometric sensors or devices, such as fingerprint scanners or facial recognition cameras, at access points or on devices that require authentication, allowing users to authenticate using their unique biometric traits. Additionally, many modern smartphones, tablets, and laptops come equipped with built-in biometric sensors, enabling users to authenticate using features like Touch ID or Face ID. Another widely used form of MFA is SMS-based authentication, which sends a one-time code to the user's mobile phone via SMS message, requiring them to enter the code along with their password to complete the authentication process. While SMS-based MFA is convenient and widely supported, it is susceptible to interception or SIM swapping attacks, where attackers gain access to the user's phone number and intercept SMS messages containing authentication codes, highlighting the importance of using more secure MFA methods whenever possible. Organizations can implement MFA using various authentication methods depending on their security requirements and user preferences, often combining multiple factors for added security. For example, a system might require users to enter a password (something they know) along with a code generated by a mobile authenticator app (something they have) or a fingerprint scan (something they are) to authenticate successfully, providing multiple layers of protection against unauthorized access. Additionally, MFA can be integrated with single sign-on (SSO) solutions to provide seamless access to multiple applications and services while still maintaining strong authentication controls. SSO allows users to log in once with their credentials and access multiple applications without needing to re-enter their password each time, improving user experience without sacrificing security. However, it's essential for organizations to implement MFA properly to avoid common pitfalls and ensure effective security controls. This includes educating users about the importance of MFA and how to use it correctly, providing clear instructions for setting up and using MFA methods, and regularly reviewing and updating MFA policies and configurations to address emerging threats and vulnerabilities. By implementing MFA effectively, organizations can significantly reduce the risk of unauthorized access, data breaches, and account compromise, enhancing overall security posture and protecting sensitive information from unauthorized access.*

Cloud Network Architecture refers to the design and layout of networking components and infrastructure within cloud computing environments, encompassing the configuration, connectivity, and management of network resources to support the delivery of cloud-based services and applications. Cloud network architecture plays a crucial role in determining the performance, scalability, and security of cloud-based solutions, providing the foundation for communication and data exchange between cloud resources, end-users, and external networks. One key aspect of cloud network architecture is the design of virtual networks, which enable organizations to create isolated network environments within the cloud to segment workloads, applications, and data, providing enhanced security and performance isolation. Virtual networks are typically implemented using virtual private cloud (VPC) or virtual network (VNet) services provided by cloud service providers such as Amazon Web Services (AWS), Microsoft Azure, or Google Cloud Platform (GCP), allowing organizations to define custom network topologies, subnets, and routing configurations to meet their specific requirements. To create a virtual network in

AWS, for example, organizations can use the AWS Management Console or AWS Command Line Interface (CLI) to define a VPC with the desired CIDR block and subnet configurations, specifying the availability zones and route tables for routing traffic between subnets and external networks. Another essential component of cloud network architecture is the deployment of network security controls, such as firewalls, network access control lists (ACLs), and security groups, to protect cloud resources from unauthorized access, network threats, and malicious activities. These security controls help enforce security policies and restrict inbound and outbound traffic based on predefined rules, allowing organizations to control access to cloud resources and prevent unauthorized access or data breaches. In AWS, organizations can use security groups to define inbound and outbound traffic rules for EC2 instances, specifying the allowed protocols, ports, and IP addresses or CIDR blocks that are permitted to communicate with the instances. Additionally, organizations can configure network ACLs at the subnet level to filter traffic based on IP addresses, port numbers, and protocols, providing an additional layer of security at the network perimeter. Cloud network architecture also involves the deployment of networking services and technologies to optimize performance, reliability, and scalability, such as content delivery networks

(CDNs), load balancers, and virtual private networks (VPNs). CDNs improve the delivery of web content and applications by caching content at edge locations closer to end-users, reducing latency and improving responsiveness. Load balancers distribute incoming traffic across multiple backend servers or instances to ensure high availability, fault tolerance, and scalability of cloud-based applications. VPNs establish secure encrypted connections between on-premises networks and cloud environments, enabling secure remote access and data exchange over public networks such as the internet. Organizations can deploy these networking services and technologies using cloud-native services provided by cloud service providers or third-party solutions integrated with cloud platforms, configuring settings and parameters to optimize performance and meet specific business requirements. Additionally, cloud network architecture includes considerations for network monitoring, management, and optimization, enabling organizations to monitor network performance, troubleshoot connectivity issues, and optimize resource utilization to improve overall efficiency and cost-effectiveness. Cloud-native monitoring and management tools, such as AWS CloudWatch, Azure Monitor, or Google Cloud Monitoring, provide visibility into network traffic, performance metrics, and resource utilization,

allowing organizations to identify and address potential issues proactively. These tools also support automation and orchestration of network resources, enabling organizations to scale network capacity up or down dynamically in response to changing demand or workload requirements. In summary, cloud network architecture plays a critical role in the design and operation of cloud computing environments, providing the infrastructure and connectivity required to deliver cloud-based services and applications effectively. By implementing best practices for virtual network design, network security, performance optimization, and monitoring, organizations can build resilient, scalable, and secure cloud network architectures that meet their business needs and objectives. Secure Cloud Connectivity is a fundamental aspect of cloud computing that focuses on establishing secure connections between on-premises networks, cloud environments, and external networks to ensure the confidentiality, integrity, and availability of data and services transmitted over the network. Secure cloud connectivity involves implementing robust security measures and protocols to protect data in transit and prevent unauthorized access or interception of sensitive information. One key component of secure cloud connectivity is the use of virtual private networks (VPNs) to create encrypted tunnels between on-premises networks and cloud environments, allowing organizations to establish secure and private communication channels over public networks such as the internet. VPNs encrypt data packets before transmission and decrypt them upon receipt, ensuring that data remains confidential and secure while traversing insecure networks. To set up a VPN connection between an on-premises network and a cloud environment, organizations can use VPN gateway services provided by cloud service providers such as AWS VPN, Azure VPN Gateway, or Google Cloud VPN. These services allow organizations to deploy virtual VPN appliances or gateways in the cloud and configure VPN connections using standard protocols such as IPsec or SSL/TLS. For example, in AWS, organizations can use the AWS Management Console or AWS CLI to create a VPN connection between an AWS Virtual Private Gateway (VGW) and an on-premises VPN device, specifying the encryption algorithms, authentication methods, and pre-shared keys required for secure communication. Another aspect of secure cloud connectivity is the use of dedicated private connections, such as Direct Connect (AWS), ExpressRoute (Azure), or Cloud Interconnect (Google Cloud), to establish direct, high-bandwidth links between on-premises networks and cloud environments, bypassing the public internet and reducing exposure to external threats. These dedicated connections provide reliable, low-latency connectivity and can be used to transfer large volumes of data between on-premises and cloud environments securely. Organizations can provision dedicated connections through network service providers or colocation facilities and establish private peering relationships with cloud service providers to establish direct connectivity to their cloud networks. Additionally, secure cloud connectivity involves implementing network security controls such as firewalls, intrusion detection and prevention systems (IDPS), and network access control lists (ACLs) to protect cloud environments from unauthorized access, malware, and other security threats. These security controls help enforce security policies and restrict inbound and outbound traffic based on predefined rules, allowing organizations to control access to cloud resources and prevent unauthorized access or data breaches. In AWS, organizations can use security groups and network ACLs to define firewall rules and access control policies for EC2 instances and other cloud resources, specifying the allowed protocols, ports, and IP addresses or CIDR blocks that are permitted to communicate with the instances. Moreover, secure cloud connectivity requires implementing robust authentication and authorization mechanisms to verify the identities of users and devices accessing cloud resources and enforce access controls based on their roles and permissions.

Organizations can use identity and access management (IAM) services provided by cloud service providers to manage user identities, define access policies, and authenticate users using methods such as username/password authentication, multi-factor authentication (MFA), or federated identity providers. For example, in Azure, organizations can use Azure Active Directory (Azure AD) to manage user identities and access permissions for Azure resources, enabling single sign-on (SSO) and integrating with external identity providers such as Active Directory Federation Services (ADFS) or SAML-based identity providers. Additionally, secure cloud connectivity involves implementing encryption mechanisms such as Transport Layer Security (TLS) or IPsec to protect data transmitted over the network and prevent eavesdropping or tampering by unauthorized parties. Organizations can use TLS to encrypt data transmitted between clients and cloud services over the internet, ensuring that data remains confidential and secure during transmission. Similarly, IPsec can be used to create encrypted tunnels between cloud environments and external networks, providing end-to-end encryption for data in transit and protecting against interception or manipulation of data packets. In summary, secure cloud connectivity is essential for ensuring the confidentiality, integrity, and availability of data and services in cloud computing environments. By implementing robust security measures such as VPNs, dedicated connections, network security controls, authentication and authorization mechanisms, and encryption protocols, organizations can establish secure and reliable connections between on-premises networks and cloud environments, enabling seamless communication and collaboration while protecting against external threats and security vulnerabilities.

Data Classification and Handling is a critical aspect of information security that involves categorizing data based on its sensitivity, importance, and regulatory requirements, and implementing appropriate controls and safeguards to protect it from unauthorized access, disclosure, or misuse. Data classification helps organizations identify and prioritize their data assets, enabling them to allocate resources effectively and apply security controls commensurate with the value and risk associated with different types of data. One common approach to data classification is to categorize data into different levels or tiers based on its sensitivity and confidentiality requirements, such as public, internal, confidential, or restricted. Each data classification level is associated with specific handling requirements and security controls to ensure that data is adequately protected throughout its lifecycle. To classify data effectively, organizations can use automated tools or manual processes to analyze data attributes such as content, context, and usage patterns and assign appropriate classification labels based on predefined criteria or policies. For example, organizations can use data loss prevention (DLP) solutions to scan and analyze data at rest, in motion, or in use and apply classification labels based on predefined rules or patterns, such as detecting sensitive information like personally identifiable information (PII), financial data, or intellectual property. Once data has been classified, organizations must establish clear policies and procedures for handling and managing data according to its classification level, outlining guidelines for access control, encryption, retention, and disposal based on the sensitivity and regulatory requirements of the data. Access control mechanisms such as role-based access control (RBAC) or attribute-based access control (ABAC) can be used to enforce access restrictions and permissions based on the data classification level and the roles and responsibilities of users within the organization. For example, organizations can use access control lists (ACLs) or group policies to restrict access to confidential or sensitive data to authorized users or groups and enforce encryption requirements for data in transit or storage. Additionally, organizations should implement data encryption techniques such as encryption at rest and encryption in transit to protect data from unauthorized access or interception. Encryption at rest involves encrypting data stored on disk or in databases using encryption algorithms and cryptographic keys to prevent unauthorized access or data theft in the event of a security breach or unauthorized access to storage devices. In a Linux environment, organizations can use tools like OpenSSL or GnuPG to encrypt sensitive files or directories using symmetric or asymmetric encryption algorithms, specifying encryption parameters such as key length, cipher suite, and passphrase. Encryption in transit involves encrypting data as it travels between endpoints or across networks to prevent eavesdropping or interception by unauthorized parties. Organizations can use protocols such as Transport Layer Security (TLS) or Secure Shell (SSH) to encrypt data transmitted over the internet or private networks, ensuring that data remains confidential and secure during transmission. Data classification and handling also involve implementing data retention and disposal policies to ensure that data is retained for only as long as necessary and securely disposed of when no longer needed. Organizations should establish clear guidelines for data retention periods based on regulatory requirements, business needs, and legal considerations, outlining procedures for archiving or deleting data at the end of its lifecycle. For example, organizations can use data lifecycle management (DLM) tools or archival solutions to automatically archive data to long-term storage repositories or delete data that has reached the end of its retention period, ensuring compliance with data protection regulations and minimizing the risk of data breaches or unauthorized access to obsolete data. Additionally, organizations should implement secure deletion techniques such as data wiping or shredding to permanently erase data from storage devices and prevent data recovery by unauthorized parties. In a Linux environment, organizations can use utilities like shred or wipe to securely erase files or disk partitions by overwriting them with random data multiple times, making it virtually impossible to recover the original data. Overall, effective data classification and handling are essential for protecting sensitive information, ensuring regulatory compliance, and mitigating the risk of data breaches or unauthorized access. By implementing robust classification policies, access controls, encryption techniques, and data retention and disposal procedures, organizations can safeguard their data assets and maintain the confidentiality, integrity, and availability of data throughout its lifecycle.

Privacy Regulations and Compliance are crucial aspects of information governance and data protection that govern how organizations collect, process, store, and share personal information, and ensure that individuals' privacy rights are protected. Privacy regulations establish legal requirements and standards for handling personal data, including sensitive information such as personally identifiable *information (PII), health records, financial data, and biometric data, and impose obligations on organizations to safeguard the privacy and security of this information. One of the most well-known privacy regulations is the General Data Protection Regulation (GDPR), which was introduced by the European Union (EU) to harmonize data protection laws across EU member states and regulate the processing of personal data by businesses and organizations operating within the EU or targeting EU residents. The GDPR imposes strict requirements on organizations regarding consent, transparency, data minimization, purpose limitation, accountability, and individuals' rights, such as the right to access, rectify, and erase personal data, the right to data portability, and the right to be informed about data processing activities. To comply with the GDPR, organizations must implement measures to ensure the lawful and fair processing of personal data, including obtaining explicit consent from individuals before collecting their data, providing clear and transparent privacy notices detailing how personal data will be used, and implementing appropriate technical and organizational security measures to protect personal data from unauthorized access, disclosure, alteration, or destruction. For example, organizations can use data encryption, access controls, pseudonymization, and anonymization techniques to protect personal data from unauthorized access or disclosure, and implement data protection impact assessments (DPIAs) to identify and mitigate privacy risks associated with data processing activities. Another important privacy regulation is the California Consumer Privacy Act (CCPA), which was enacted by the state of California to enhance privacy rights and consumer protections for California residents and regulate the collection, use, and sale of personal information by businesses operating in California. The CCPA grants California residents certain rights regarding their personal information, including the right to know what personal information is being collected about them, the right to opt-out of the sale of their personal information, and the right to request the deletion of their personal information. To comply with the CCPA, organizations must provide consumers with clear and conspicuous privacy notices disclosing their data collection practices, inform consumers about their rights under the CCPA, and establish processes for responding to consumer requests regarding their personal information, such as providing access to or deleting personal data upon request. Additionally, organizations must implement reasonable security measures to protect personal information from unauthorized access, disclosure, or misuse, and refrain from selling personal information without the explicit consent of the consumer. To comply with the CCPA's requirement to provide consumers with the right to opt-out of the sale of their personal information, organizations can implement mechanisms such as "Do Not Sell My Personal Information" links on their websites or mobile applications, allowing consumers to exercise their opt-out rights easily. Furthermore, organizations must update their privacy policies and procedures regularly to reflect changes in privacy laws and regulations and ensure ongoing compliance with applicable requirements. In addition to the GDPR and CCPA, there are numerous other privacy regulations and frameworks around the world that organizations may need to comply with, depending on their geographic location, industry, and the nature of their data processing activities. For example, in the healthcare industry, organizations must comply with the Health Insurance Portability and Accountability Act (HIPAA) in the United States, which regulates the privacy and security of protected health information (PHI) and imposes requirements on healthcare providers, health plans, and healthcare clearinghouses to safeguard the confidentiality and integrity of PHI. Similarly, in the financial services industry, organizations must comply with regulations such as the Payment Card Industry Data Security Standard (PCI DSS) for credit card data security and the Sarbanes-Oxley Act (SOX) for financial reporting and corporate governance. To ensure compliance with privacy regulations and frameworks, organizations should conduct regular audits and assessments of their privacy practices and controls, identify gaps and deficiencies, and implement remediation measures to address non-compliance issues and mitigate privacy risks. Additionally, organizations should invest in privacy training and awareness programs to educate employees about their privacy obligations and responsibilities and foster a culture of privacy and data protection throughout the organization. By prioritizing privacy compliance and implementing robust privacy management practices, organizations can build trust with consumers, reduce the risk of regulatory penalties and fines, and protect their reputation and brand integrity in an increasingly data-driven world.*

Cloud Compliance Frameworks are essential tools for organizations operating in cloud environments to ensure that their cloud-based services and solutions comply with regulatory requirements, industry standards, and best practices for security, privacy, and governance. These frameworks provide guidance, controls, and recommendations for designing, implementing, and managing cloud environments in a compliant manner, helping organizations address legal, regulatory, and contractual obligations while leveraging the benefits of cloud computing. One widely adopted cloud compliance framework is the Cloud Security Alliance (CSA) Cloud Controls Matrix (CCM), which provides a comprehensive set of security controls mapped to leading industry standards and frameworks, such as ISO/IEC 27001, NIST Cybersecurity Framework, and PCI DSS, to help organizations assess the security posture of their cloud environments and demonstrate compliance with regulatory requirements. The CCM covers various domains, including governance and risk management, legal and regulatory compliance, data security, identity and access management, and incident response, providing organizations with a holistic approach to cloud security and compliance. To implement the CSA CCM, organizations can use the

CSA's self-assessment tools or engage third-party auditors to assess their compliance with the framework's control objectives and requirements, identify gaps and deficiencies, and develop remediation plans to address non-compliance issues. Another widely recognized cloud compliance framework is the International Organization for Standardization (ISO) 27001 standard, which provides a globally recognized framework for establishing, implementing, maintaining, and continually improving an information security management system (ISMS). ISO 27001 sets out requirements for identifying, assessing, and managing information security risks, implementing controls to mitigate risks, and monitoring and reviewing the effectiveness of security measures, helping organizations protect the confidentiality, integrity, and availability of information assets. To achieve ISO 27001 certification for cloud environments, organizations must undergo a rigorous certification process that involves conducting a risk assessment, developing an ISMS based on ISO 27001 requirements, implementing security controls and measures to address identified risks, and undergoing audits and assessments by accredited certification bodies to verify compliance with the standard's requirements. Additionally, organizations can leverage industry-specific compliance frameworks and regulations tailored to their sector or industry, such as the Health Insurance Portability and Accountability Act (HIPAA) for healthcare organizations, the Payment Card Industry Data Security Standard (PCI DSS) for payment card industry, and the General Data Protection Regulation (GDPR) for organizations handling personal data of EU residents. These frameworks provide specific requirements and guidelines for protecting sensitive information, ensuring data privacy and security, and complying with regulatory obligations relevant to the industry. To achieve compliance with industry-specific regulations and frameworks, organizations must implement appropriate security controls, policies, and procedures tailored to their unique regulatory requirements and business needs, such as implementing encryption for data protection, establishing access controls and audit trails for data access and usage, and conducting regular security assessments and audits to identify and address compliance gaps. Additionally, organizations can use cloud compliance management platforms and tools to automate compliance monitoring, reporting, and remediation processes, enabling them to streamline compliance efforts, reduce manual efforts and errors, and demonstrate ongoing compliance with regulatory requirements and industry standards. These platforms provide features such as policy management, risk assessment, control monitoring, audit trails, and reporting capabilities to help organizations track compliance status, identify areas of non-compliance, and take corrective actions to address deficiencies and vulnerabilities. Furthermore, organizations can leverage cloud service provider (CSP) compliance certifications and attestations to demonstrate compliance with industry standards and regulatory requirements. Leading CSPs, such as Amazon Web Services (AWS), Microsoft Azure, and Google Cloud Platform (GCP), undergo independent third-party audits and assessments to certify their compliance with industry standards, such as ISO 27001, SOC 2, HIPAA, and GDPR, and provide customers with assurance that their cloud services meet stringent security and compliance requirements. To verify CSP compliance certifications, organizations can request audit reports, certificates, and other compliance documentation from their CSPs and review them to ensure alignment with their own compliance requirements and obligations. In summary, cloud compliance frameworks play a vital role in helping organizations establish and maintain compliant cloud environments by providing guidance, controls, and recommendations for addressing regulatory requirements, industry standards, and best practices for security, privacy, and governance. By leveraging these frameworks, organizations can strengthen their security posture, protect sensitive information, mitigate risks, and demonstrate compliance with legal, regulatory, and contractual obligations, thereby building trust with customers, partners, and stakeholders and ensuring the integrity and reliability of their cloud-based services and solutions. International Data Protection Laws are legal frameworks established by governments and regulatory authorities to govern the collection, processing, storage, and transfer of personal data across national borders and ensure the privacy rights and data protection of individuals worldwide. These laws are designed to regulate the handling of personal data by organizations operating globally and establish standards and requirements for the lawful and responsible use of personal information, regardless of where it is processed or stored. One of the most prominent international data protection laws is the General Data Protection Regulation (GDPR), which was introduced by the European Union (EU) in 2018 to harmonize data protection laws across EU member states and strengthen the privacy rights of EU residents. The GDPR imposes strict requirements on organizations regarding the collection, processing, and storage of personal data, including requirements for obtaining explicit consent from individuals before collecting their data, providing transparent privacy notices detailing data processing activities, and implementing appropriate technical and organizational measures to protect personal data from unauthorized access, disclosure, alteration, or destruction. To comply with the GDPR, organizations must assess their data processing activities, identify and document the personal data they collect and process, and implement measures to ensure compliance with GDPR requirements, such as conducting data protection impact assessments

(DPIAs), appointing data protection officers (DPOs), and establishing data breach notification procedures. Additionally, organizations must adhere to GDPR principles such as data minimization, purpose limitation, accuracy, integrity, and confidentiality, and implement measures such as data encryption, access controls, pseudonymization, and anonymization to protect personal data and ensure its security and privacy. Another significant international data protection law is the California Consumer Privacy Act (CCPA), which was enacted by the state of California in 2018 to enhance privacy rights and consumer protections for California residents and regulate the collection, use, and sale of personal information by businesses operating in California. The CCPA grants California residents certain rights regarding their personal information, including the right to know what personal information is being collected about them, the right to opt-out of the sale of their personal information, and the right to request the deletion of their personal information. To comply with the CCPA, organizations must provide consumers with clear and conspicuous privacy notices disclosing their data collection practices, inform consumers about their rights under the CCPA, and establish processes for responding to consumer requests regarding their personal information, such as providing access to or deleting personal data upon request. Additionally, organizations must implement reasonable security measures to protect personal information from

unauthorized access, disclosure, or misuse, and refrain from selling personal information without the explicit consent of the consumer. Moreover, the Asia-Pacific region has seen the emergence of several data protection laws and regulations aimed at protecting the privacy rights of individuals and regulating the handling of personal data by organizations operating in the region. For example, the Personal Data Protection Act (PDPA) in Singapore, the Personal Information Protection Law (PIPL) in China, and the Personal Data Protection Bill in India are all aimed at establishing comprehensive data protection frameworks and standards for protecting personal data and ensuring compliance with privacy principles and obligations. These laws typically include requirements for obtaining consent for data processing, providing transparent privacy notices, implementing security measures to protect personal data, and establishing mechanisms for individuals to exercise their rights over their personal information, such as accessing, correcting, or deleting their data. To comply with these data protection laws and regulations, organizations operating in the Asia-Pacific region must conduct assessments of their data processing activities, identify and document the personal data they collect and process, and implement measures to ensure compliance with applicable requirements, such as appointing data protection officers, conducting privacy impact assessments, and implementing security controls and safeguards to protect personal data from unauthorized access, disclosure, or misuse. Additionally, organizations must establish processes and procedures for responding to data subject requests and inquiries regarding their personal information and ensure that their data processing activities are conducted in accordance with applicable laws and regulations. In summary, international data protection laws play a critical role in regulating the collection, processing, and transfer of personal data across borders and protecting the privacy rights of individuals worldwide. By complying with these laws and implementing appropriate security measures and controls, organizations can safeguard personal data, build trust with consumers, and demonstrate their commitment to protecting privacy and data protection in an increasingly interconnected and data-driven world.

A Cloud Incident Response Plan is a crucial component of an organization's cybersecurity strategy that outlines procedures and protocols for responding to security incidents and breaches in cloud environments, ensuring a timely and effective response to mitigate risks, minimize impact, and restore normal operations. The Incident Response Plan typically includes predefined steps and actions for identifying, containing, eradicating, and recovering from security incidents, as well as roles and responsibilities for incident response team members and communication protocols for notifying stakeholders and authorities. To develop a Cloud Incident Response Plan, organizations must first conduct a risk assessment to identify potential threats and vulnerabilities in their cloud environments, such as unauthorized access, data breaches, malware infections, or denial-of-service (DoS) attacks, and evaluate the potential impact of these incidents on their business operations and data assets. Once risks are identified, organizations can develop incident response procedures and guidelines tailored to their specific cloud infrastructure, applications, and data, outlining steps for detecting, analyzing, and responding to security incidents in a systematic and coordinated manner. For example, organizations can use cloud-native monitoring and logging tools provided by cloud service providers (CSPs) to monitor and analyze activity logs, network traffic, and system events in their cloud environments, enabling them to detect and investigate security incidents in real-time. AWS CloudTrail, Azure Monitor, and Google Cloud Audit Logs are examples of cloud logging and monitoring services that organizations can leverage to track user activity, API calls, and resource changes in their cloud environments and identify potential security threats or anomalies. In addition to monitoring and logging, organizations should implement incident detection and alerting mechanisms to notify incident response team members of potential security incidents and trigger immediate response actions. For example, organizations can configure intrusion detection and prevention systems (IDPS), security information and event management (SIEM) solutions, or cloud-native security services such as AWS GuardDuty, Azure Security Center, or Google Cloud Security Command Center to automatically detect and alert on suspicious activities or security events in their cloud environments. These systems can generate alerts based on predefined rules, thresholds, or anomaly detection algorithms and notify incident response team members via email, SMS, or pager notifications, enabling them to investigate and respond to security incidents promptly. Once a security incident is detected, organizations must follow predefined incident response procedures to contain the incident and prevent further damage or unauthorized access to cloud resources and data. This may involve isolating affected systems or networks, disabling compromised user accounts, revoking access privileges, or blocking malicious IP addresses or domains to prevent further attacks or data exfiltration. For example, organizations can use cloud security group rules, network access control lists (ACLs), or web application firewalls (WAFs) to restrict inbound and outbound traffic to and from compromised resources, preventing attackers from exploiting vulnerabilities or accessing sensitive data. Additionally, organizations should preserve evidence and forensic data related to the security incident to support post-incident analysis and investigation and facilitate legal or regulatory reporting requirements. This may include capturing memory dumps, disk images, network packet captures, and log files from affected systems and storing them in a secure, tamper-evident manner to maintain their integrity and chain of custody. Cloud incident response teams should also communicate with internal stakeholders, external partners, and regulatory authorities as necessary to coordinate response efforts, share relevant information, and comply with legal and regulatory obligations. This may involve notifying senior management, legal counsel, public relations teams, and law enforcement agencies, as well as affected customers, vendors, and partners, depending on the severity and impact of the security incident. Effective communication is essential for maintaining transparency, managing stakeholder expectations, and preserving the organization's reputation and credibility during and after a security incident. After the security incident has been contained and mitigated, organizations should conduct a post-incident review and analysis to identify lessons learned, root causes, and areas for improvement in their incident response procedures and controls. This may involve conducting a comprehensive post-mortem analysis of the incident, documenting findings, and developing recommendations for enhancing incident detection, response, and recovery capabilities in the future. By continuously evaluating and refining their Cloud Incident Response Plan, organizations can strengthen their cybersecurity posture, improve their ability to detect and respond to security incidents, and minimize the impact of cyber threats on their cloud environments and business operations.

Cloud Disaster Recovery Strategies are essential components of a comprehensive business continuity plan that organizations implement to ensure the resilience and availability of their critical systems and data in the event of unforeseen disasters or disruptions. These strategies involve deploying redundant infrastructure, data replication, and failover mechanisms in cloud environments to minimize downtime, data loss, and service disruptions and facilitate rapid recovery and resumption of business operations following a disaster. One common cloud disaster recovery strategy is to leverage cloud-based backup and replication services to replicate critical data and applications to geographically dispersed cloud regions or data centers, ensuring data redundancy and availability across multiple locations. For example, organizations can use AWS Backup, Azure Site Recovery, or Google Cloud Storage to back up and replicate data and virtual machines (VMs) from on-premises environments to cloud storage repositories or virtualized instances in remote regions, enabling them to restore data and applications quickly in the event of a disaster. To deploy these services, organizations must first configure backup policies and replication settings, specifying the frequency of data replication, retention periods, and target regions or data centers for storing backup copies. For example, in AWS Backup, organizations can use the create-backup-plan and create-backup-selection commands to create backup plans and select resources to be backed up, specifying parameters such as backup frequency, retention periods, and backup vault settings. Similarly, in Azure Site Recovery, organizations can use the Set-AzRecoveryServicesAsrPolicy and Set-AzRecoveryServicesAsrProtectionContainerMapping commands to configure replication policies and protection container mappings, defining replication settings such as recovery point objectives (RPOs), recovery time objectives (RTOs), and target regions for failover. Once backup and replication policies are configured, organizations can initiate initial data replication and synchronization processes to replicate data from on-premises environments to cloud storage repositories or virtualized instances in remote regions. For example, in Google Cloud Storage, organizations can use the gsutil rsync command to synchronize data between on-premises storage systems and cloud storage buckets, ensuring that backup copies are up-to-date and consistent with production data. Additionally, organizations should conduct regular tests and drills of their cloud disaster recovery plans to validate the effectiveness and reliability of their recovery procedures and identify any gaps or deficiencies that need to be addressed. For example, organizations can use AWS Disaster Recovery Testing, Azure Site Recovery Recovery Plans, or

Google Cloud Disaster Recovery Drills to simulate disaster scenarios, failover applications and services to remote regions or data centers, and validate recovery time objectives (RTOs) and recovery point objectives (RPOs). By conducting regular tests and drills, organizations can identify and remediate issues proactively, optimize recovery procedures, and ensure that they can recover critical systems and data within the desired timeframes in the event of a real disaster. In addition to backup and replication, organizations can implement disaster recovery as a service (DRaaS) solutions offered by cloud service providers to automate and orchestrate the failover and failback of critical workloads and applications in the event of a disaster. These DRaaS solutions typically include features such as automated failover, continuous data replication, application consistency, and network connectivity orchestration to ensure seamless failover and recovery of workloads across geographically dispersed cloud regions or data centers. For example, organizations can use AWS Disaster Recovery, Azure Site Recovery, or Google Cloud DRaaS to replicate VMs, databases, and applications from on-premises environments to cloud environments, configure failover policies and recovery plans, and automate the failover and failback processes in the event of a disaster. To deploy DRaaS solutions, organizations must first assess their recovery requirements, define recovery objectives, and identify critical workloads and applications that require protection and failover capabilities. Once requirements are defined, organizations can configure replication settings, recovery plans, and failover policies, specifying parameters such as recovery point objectives (RPOs), recovery time objectives (RTOs), and target regions or data centers for failover. After configuring DRaaS settings, organizations can initiate initial data replication and synchronization processes to replicate data and applications from on-premises environments to cloud environments, ensuring data redundancy and availability for failover and recovery. Additionally, organizations should monitor and manage their cloud disaster recovery solutions proactively, regularly monitoring replication status, performance metrics, and health checks to ensure that replication processes are running smoothly, data integrity is maintained, and failover capabilities are up-to-date and reliable. For example, organizations can use AWS CloudWatch, Azure Monitor, or Google Cloud Operations to monitor replication status, track performance metrics, and receive alerts and notifications in real-time regarding replication failures, latency issues, or other potential issues that may impact disaster recovery operations. By monitoring and managing their cloud disaster recovery solutions effectively, organizations can identify and address issues proactively, optimize performance, and ensure the availability and reliability of their disaster recovery capabilities to minimize downtime and data loss in the event of a disaster.

The CCSP Exam Overview provides aspiring candidates with a comprehensive understanding of the Certified Cloud Security Professional (CCSP) certification exam, covering exam objectives, format, content domains, and preparation strategies to help candidates prepare effectively and succeed in their certification journey. The CCSP exam is designed to validate candidates' knowledge and skills in cloud security architecture, design, operations, and compliance, demonstrating their expertise in securing cloud environments and protecting cloud-based assets, data, and applications from cybersecurity threats and risks. The CCSP exam is administered by (ISC)², a globally recognized nonprofit organization that specializes in cybersecurity education and certification, and is accredited by the American National Standards Institute (ANSI) to meet rigorous standards for quality and credibility. The CCSP exam consists of 125 multiple-choice questions, with a time limit of four hours to complete the exam, and is delivered through Pearson VUE test centers worldwide or via remote proctoring options, allowing candidates to take the exam online from their preferred location. To register for the CCSP exam, candidates must create an account on the (ISC)² website, pay the exam registration fee, and schedule their exam appointment through the Pearson VUE website, selecting a convenient test center location and date for their exam. The CCSP exam covers six domains of cloud security knowledge and skills, as defined by the (ISC)² Common Body of Knowledge (CBK), including Cloud Concepts, Architecture, and Design; Cloud Data Security; Cloud Platform and Infrastructure Security; Cloud Application Security; Cloud Security Operations; and Legal, Risk, and Compliance. Each domain represents a specific area of cloud security expertise and includes a set of exam objectives and knowledge areas that candidates are required to master to pass the exam and earn the CCSP certification. To prepare for the CCSP exam, candidates can use various study resources and preparation materials provided by (ISC)², such as official study guides, practice tests, and training courses, as well as third-party study materials and resources from reputable cybersecurity training providers. Additionally, candidates can participate in online forums, study groups, and community discussions to share insights, tips, and study strategies with fellow candidates and learn from their experiences preparing for the exam. When studying for the CCSP exam, candidates should focus on mastering key concepts, principles, and best practices in cloud security, such as cloud computing models and service delivery models, cloud architecture and design principles, data protection and encryption techniques, identity and access management (IAM), security controls and measures for securing cloud platforms and infrastructure, secure development practices for cloud-based applications, cloud security operations and incident response procedures, and legal and regulatory requirements for cloud compliance and governance. Candidates should also familiarize themselves with the (ISC)² Code of Ethics and adhere to ethical principles and professional standards when preparing for and taking the CCSP exam, ensuring the integrity and credibility of the certification process and upholding the reputation of the cybersecurity profession. During the exam, candidates should carefully read and analyze each question, identify keywords and key phrases, and eliminate incorrect answer choices to narrow down their options and make informed decisions when selecting the best answer. Candidates should also manage their time effectively, pacing themselves throughout the exam to ensure they have enough time to complete all questions and review their answers before submitting their exam for scoring. After completing the exam, candidates will receive a preliminary pass or fail result on the screen, indicating whether they have met the passing score threshold to earn the CCSP certification. Candidates who pass the exam will receive their official score report and certification notification from (ISC)² via email within a few weeks of taking the exam, while candidates who fail the exam can retake the exam after a waiting period of 30 days, up to three times within a 12-month period, to achieve a passing score and earn the CCSP certification.

Study Strategies and Resources are essential components of a successful learning journey, providing learners with effective techniques and materials to enhance their understanding, retention, and application of knowledge in various subject areas. When preparing for exams or learning new skills, it's crucial to develop a strategic study plan that aligns with your goals, learning style, and schedule, enabling you to maximize your learning outcomes and achieve your objectives. One effective study strategy is to create a study schedule or timetable that outlines specific study sessions, topics, and activities to cover each day or week, helping you stay organized, focused, and on track with your learning goals. By allocating dedicated time for studying and review, you can ensure consistent progress and avoid procrastination or cramming before exams or deadlines, increasing your retention and understanding of the material over time. Additionally, incorporating active learning techniques such as summarizing, questioning, and self-testing into your study routine can enhance your comprehension and retention of key concepts and information. For example, you can use techniques like the Feynman technique to explain complex topics or concepts in simple terms, teach them to someone else, or create flashcards or quizzes to test your knowledge and reinforce your understanding. Another effective study strategy is to leverage a variety of study resources and materials to supplement your learning and gain diverse perspectives on the subject matter. This may include textbooks, online courses, video lectures, academic journals, research papers, and study guides, as well as interactive learning platforms, practice exams, and study groups or forums where you can engage with peers and instructors, ask questions, and exchange ideas. When selecting study resources, it's essential to choose materials that are relevant, accurate, and up-to-date with the latest information and developments in the field, ensuring that you're learning from credible sources and staying informed about current trends and best practices. Additionally, using multiple sources of information can help reinforce your understanding of complex topics and expose you to different viewpoints and approaches to problem-solving, expanding your knowledge and critical thinking skills. When studying technical subjects or preparing for certification exams, hands-on practice and real-world application are essential for mastering skills and building proficiency. One effective way to gain practical experience is to use virtual labs or cloud-based environments to simulate real-world scenarios and practice applying concepts and techniques in a controlled setting. For example, you can use virtualization software such as VMware or VirtualBox to create virtual machines (VMs) and networks, install operating systems and applications, and configure security settings and policies to simulate various IT environments and scenarios. Additionally, cloud platforms like AWS, Azure, and

Google Cloud offer free-tier accounts and sandbox environments where you can deploy virtual machines, containers, and services to practice cloud computing concepts and experiment with different cloud technologies and services. By gaining hands-on experience through practical labs and exercises, you can reinforce your theoretical knowledge, develop problem-solving skills, and build confidence in your ability to apply what you've learned in real-world situations. Another valuable study resource is practice exams or mock tests, which simulate the format, structure, and content of the actual exam and help you assess your readiness and identify areas for improvement. Many certification programs and online learning platforms offer practice exams and sample questions to help candidates prepare for exams and gauge their proficiency in the subject matter. By taking practice exams regularly and reviewing your performance, you can identify weak areas, focus your study efforts on topics that require more attention, and track your progress over time, increasing your confidence and readiness for the actual exam. Additionally, participating in study groups or study buddies can provide valuable support, motivation, and accountability throughout your learning journey, enabling you to share resources, exchange ideas, and collaborate with peers who are also preparing for the same exam or pursuing similar learning goals. By collaborating with others, you can leverage collective knowledge and expertise, gain new insights and perspectives, and stay motivated and engaged in your studies, increasing your chances of success and achievement. In summary, effective study strategies and resources are essential for maximizing learning outcomes, enhancing understanding and retention, and achieving success in exams and learning goals. By developing a strategic study plan, leveraging diverse study resources, gaining hands-on experience through practical labs and exercises, and participating in collaborative learning activities, you can optimize your learning process, overcome challenges, and achieve your desired outcomes in your academic and professional pursuits.

BOOK 2
SECURING CLOUD INFRASTRUCTURE
ADVANCED TECHNIQUES FOR CCSP

ROB BOTWRIGHT

Cloud Security Architecture Design is a critical aspect of building secure and resilient cloud environments, encompassing the planning, implementation, and management of security controls, mechanisms, and best practices to protect cloud-based assets, data, and applications from cybersecurity threats and risks. When designing cloud security architectures, organizations must consider various factors, including their business requirements, compliance obligations, risk tolerance, and the unique characteristics and challenges of cloud computing environments. One fundamental principle of cloud security architecture design is the concept of defense-in-depth, which involves implementing multiple layers of security controls and safeguards to provide overlapping layers of protection and mitigate the impact of security breaches or incidents. By adopting a layered approach to security, organizations can enhance their resilience to cyber threats and reduce the likelihood of successful attacks against their cloud infrastructure and resources. To design an effective cloud security architecture, organizations should start by conducting a comprehensive risk assessment to identify potential threats, vulnerabilities, and risks in their cloud environments and evaluate the potential impact of these risks on their business operations and objectives. This may involve assessing the security posture of cloud service providers (CSPs), evaluating the security controls and measures implemented by CSPs to protect cloud infrastructure and services, and identifying gaps or deficiencies in existing security controls that need to be addressed. Once risks are identified, organizations can develop a risk management strategy and mitigation plan to prioritize and address the most critical risks and implement appropriate security controls and countermeasures to mitigate these risks effectively. One essential aspect of cloud security architecture design is establishing robust identity and access management (IAM) controls to govern and control access to cloud resources and services. IAM controls help organizations enforce the principle of least privilege, ensuring that users and entities have only the minimum level of access required to perform their authorized tasks and reducing the risk of unauthorized access or privilege escalation. To implement IAM controls in cloud environments, organizations can use cloud-native IAM services provided by CSPs, such as AWS Identity and Access Management (IAM), Azure Active Directory (AD), or Google Cloud Identity and Access Management (IAM), to create and manage user accounts, groups, roles, and permissions, and enforce access policies and restrictions based on user roles, job functions, and organizational hierarchies. Additionally, organizations can use multi-factor *authentication (MFA), single sign-on (SSO), and federated identity management (FIM) solutions to enhance authentication and authorization mechanisms and protect against unauthorized access and credential theft. Another critical aspect of cloud security architecture design is implementing encryption and data protection mechanisms to safeguard sensitive data and information assets stored or transmitted in cloud environments. Encryption helps organizations protect data confidentiality and integrity by encoding data in such a way that only authorized parties with the appropriate decryption keys can access and decipher the encrypted information. To implement encryption in cloud environments, organizations can use encryption algorithms and protocols such as Advanced Encryption Standard (AES), Transport Layer Security (TLS), or Secure Sockets Layer (SSL) to encrypt data at rest and in transit, ensuring that data is protected from unauthorized access or interception. Additionally, organizations can use cloud-native encryption services provided by CSPs, such as AWS Key Management Service (KMS), Azure Key Vault, or Google Cloud Key Management Service (KMS), to manage encryption keys and perform cryptographic operations, such as key generation, encryption, decryption, and key rotation, securely. By implementing encryption and data protection mechanisms, organizations can reduce the risk of data breaches and unauthorized access to sensitive information, comply with regulatory requirements, and enhance trust and confidence in their cloud security posture. In addition to IAM controls and encryption, organizations should implement network security controls and measures to protect cloud infrastructure and applications from network-based attacks and threats. This may involve configuring network security groups (NSGs), firewalls, and access control lists (ACLs) to restrict inbound and outbound traffic to and from cloud resources, segmenting network traffic into separate security zones or virtual networks, and implementing intrusion detection and prevention systems (IDPS) or network-based threat detection solutions to monitor and detect malicious activity or anomalies in network traffic. Additionally, organizations can use cloud-native network security services provided by CSPs, such as AWS Firewall Manager, Azure Firewall, or Google Cloud Armor, to manage and enforce network security policies and controls centrally, ensuring consistent protection and compliance across their cloud environments. By implementing robust network security controls, organizations can reduce the risk of network-based attacks, such as denial-of-service (DoS) attacks, distributed denial-of-service (DDoS) attacks, or network-based intrusions, and protect cloud infrastructure and applications from unauthorized access or compromise. In summary, Cloud Security Architecture Design plays a crucial role in building secure and resilient cloud environments, enabling organizations to protect their cloud-based assets, data, and applications from cybersecurity threats and risks effectively. By adopting a defense-in-depth approach to security, implementing robust IAM controls, encryption, and data protection mechanisms, and implementing network security controls, organizations can enhance their security posture, reduce the risk of security breaches, and ensure the confidentiality, integrity, and availability of their cloud resources and services. Secure Cloud Deployment Models are essential for ensuring the confidentiality, integrity, and availability of data and resources in cloud environments, providing organizations with flexible and scalable infrastructure options while maintaining robust security controls and measures to protect against cybersecurity threats and risks. One common cloud deployment model is the public cloud, where cloud services and resources are hosted and managed by third-party cloud service providers (CSPs) and made available to customers over the internet on a pay-as-you-go basis. To deploy applications and workloads securely in public cloud environments, organizations can use cloud-native security services and features provided by CSPs, such as AWS Identity and Access Management (IAM), Azure Active Directory (AD), or Google Cloud Identity and Access Management (IAM), to enforce access controls and permissions and manage user identities and credentials securely. Additionally, organizations can use encryption and* data protection mechanisms, such as AWS Key Management Service (KMS), Azure Key Vault, or Google Cloud Key Management Service (KMS), to encrypt sensitive data at rest and in transit and protect against unauthorized access or disclosure. Another common cloud deployment model is the private cloud, where cloud services and resources are dedicated to a single organization and hosted either on-premises or in a third-party data center, providing organizations with greater control, customization, and security over their cloud infrastructure and data. To deploy applications and workloads securely in private cloud environments, organizations can implement network segmentation, access controls, and firewall rules to restrict access to cloud resources and prevent unauthorized users or entities from accessing sensitive data or services. Additionally, organizations can use virtual private networks (VPNs) or dedicated network connections to establish secure and encrypted communication channels between on-premises environments and private cloud infrastructure, ensuring data privacy and integrity during transmission. A hybrid cloud deployment model combines elements of both public and private clouds, allowing organizations to leverage the benefits of both deployment models while addressing specific business requirements, regulatory compliance, or data residency considerations. To deploy applications and workloads securely in hybrid cloud environments, organizations can use cloud orchestration and *management tools, such as AWS CloudFormation, Azure Resource Manager (ARM), or Google Cloud Deployment Manager, to automate the provisioning, configuration, and management of cloud resources and services across multiple cloud environments. Additionally, organizations can use cloud security platforms and services, such as AWS Security Hub, Azure Security Center, or Google Cloud Security Command Center, to monitor and manage security posture, detect and respond to security threats and incidents, and enforce compliance with regulatory requirements and industry standards. Another emerging cloud deployment model is the multi-cloud, where organizations use multiple cloud service providers (CSPs) to host and manage their cloud infrastructure and services, enabling them to avoid vendor lock-in, mitigate risks of service outages or disruptions, and leverage best-of-breed solutions and services from different providers. To deploy applications and workloads securely in multi-cloud environments, organizations can implement cloud-agnostic security controls and measures, such as identity federation, single sign-on (SSO), and centralized security policy management, to ensure consistent security posture and compliance across multiple cloud environments. Additionally, organizations can use cloud-native security services and features provided by each CSP to address specific security requirements or challenges in different cloud environments, such as AWS CloudTrail for auditing and monitoring, Azure Security Center for threat detection and response, or Google Cloud Security Command Center for security analytics and insights. In summary, Secure Cloud Deployment Models are essential for organizations seeking to leverage the benefits of cloud computing while maintaining robust security controls and measures to protect against cybersecurity threats and risks. By implementing security best practices and leveraging cloud-native security services and features, organizations can deploy applications and workloads securely in public, private, hybrid, and multi-cloud environments, ensuring the confidentiality, integrity, and availability of their data and resources and maintaining compliance with regulatory requirements and industry standards.*

Hypervisor Security Mechanisms are fundamental components of virtualization technology, responsible for managing and isolating virtual machines (VMs) and ensuring the security and integrity of the underlying hardware and software infrastructure. Hypervisors, also known as virtual machine monitors (VMMs), are software or firmware components that create and manage virtualized environments, enabling multiple operating systems and applications to run on a single physical server or host system. There are two primary types of hypervisors: Type 1 hypervisors, also known as bare-metal hypervisors, run directly on the physical hardware of the host system, providing a thin layer of abstraction between the hardware and virtual machines. Type 2 hypervisors, also known as hosted hypervisors, run on top of a conventional operating system (OS) like Windows or Linux, allowing users to run virtual machines as processes within the host OS. Hypervisor security mechanisms are designed to protect against various threats and attacks that target virtualized environments, including unauthorized access, data breaches, malware infections, and denial-of-service (DoS) attacks. One of the key security mechanisms provided by hypervisors is virtual machine isolation, which ensures that each virtual machine is encapsulated and isolated from other VMs and the underlying host system, preventing unauthorized access or interference between VMs. To enforce virtual machine isolation, hypervisors use hardware-assisted virtualization features such as Intel VT-x or AMD-V, which provide hardware-level support for virtualization and enable hypervisors to create and manage isolated execution environments for VMs. Additionally, hypervisors use memory isolation techniques such as memory paging and address space layout randomization (ASLR) to prevent one VM from accessing or tampering with the memory of another VM or the hypervisor itself. Another important security mechanism provided by hypervisors is secure boot, which ensures the integrity and authenticity of the hypervisor and virtual machine images by verifying their digital signatures and integrity checksums during the boot process. Secure boot helps protect against bootkits, rootkits, and other malware that attempt to compromise the integrity of the boot process and gain unauthorized access to the hypervisor or VMs. To enable secure boot, hypervisors use trusted platform module (TPM) chips or secure boot firmware features built into modern CPUs to verify the integrity of the boot loader, kernel, and other critical components of the hypervisor and virtual machine images before they are loaded into memory and executed. Additionally, hypervisors use cryptographic techniques such as digital signatures, hash functions, and public-key cryptography to authenticate and validate the integrity of VM images and configuration files before they are deployed or migrated between host systems. One of the challenges in securing hypervisors is the risk of hypervisor-based attacks, where an attacker exploits vulnerabilities in the hypervisor software or hardware to gain unauthorized access to the host system or compromise the integrity of VMs. To mitigate the risk of hypervisor-based attacks, organizations should regularly update and patch hypervisor software and firmware to address known security vulnerabilities and apply security best practices such as least privilege, role-based access control (RBAC), and network segmentation to restrict access to hypervisor management interfaces and control planes. Additionally, organizations can use security monitoring and logging tools such as hypervisor-based intrusion detection systems (IDS) or security information and event management (SIEM) solutions to detect and respond to suspicious or malicious activity in virtualized environments. In summary, Hypervisor Security Mechanisms play a critical role in protecting virtualized environments from security threats and attacks by enforcing virtual machine isolation, ensuring the integrity and authenticity of VM images, and mitigating the risk of hypervisor-based attacks. By implementing security best practices and leveraging hypervisor security features and technologies, organizations can build secure and resilient virtualized infrastructures that meet their business requirements and regulatory compliance obligations.

Virtual Machine Isolation Techniques are essential for ensuring the security and integrity of virtualized environments by preventing unauthorized access or interference between virtual machines (VMs) and protecting against potential security threats and attacks. One common technique for isolating virtual machines is to use hardware-assisted virtualization features such as Intel VT-x or AMD-V, which provide hardware-level support for virtualization and enable hypervisors to create and manage isolated execution environments for VMs. These hardware features allow the hypervisor to enforce memory isolation, CPU isolation, and I/O isolation, ensuring that each VM is encapsulated and isolated from other VMs and the underlying host system. To enable hardware-assisted virtualization, organizations can use BIOS or UEFI settings to enable virtualization support in the CPU and motherboard firmware, allowing the hypervisor to leverage hardware features for virtualization. Additionally, organizations can use hypervisor-specific commands or tools to verify that hardware-assisted virtualization is enabled and functioning correctly. Another technique for isolating virtual machines is to use software-based isolation mechanisms such as namespaces, cgroups, and containers, which provide lightweight and efficient isolation of processes and resources within a single operating system instance. Containers are a type of lightweight virtualization technology that allows multiple applications or services to run in isolated environments called containers, each with its own file system, network stack, and process namespace. To deploy containers securely, organizations can use container orchestration platforms such as Kubernetes, Docker Swarm, or Amazon ECS to automate the deployment, scaling, and management of containerized applications and services, ensuring consistent security posture and compliance across the containerized environment. Additionally, organizations can use container security tools and services such as Docker Security Scanning, Kubernetes Network Policies, or AWS App Mesh to monitor and enforce security policies, detect and respond to security threats and vulnerabilities, and ensure the integrity and confidentiality of containerized workloads. Another technique for isolating virtual machines is to use network segmentation and firewall rules to restrict network traffic between VMs and control communication flows within the virtualized environment. Network segmentation divides the virtualized environment into separate network segments or security zones, each with its own network policies and access controls, to prevent unauthorized access or lateral movement of attackers within the network. To implement network segmentation, organizations can use virtual LANs (VLANs), subnetting, or software-defined networking (SDN) technologies to create isolated network segments for different types of VMs or applications. Additionally, organizations can use firewall rules and access control lists (ACLs) to filter and control inbound and outbound traffic to and from VMs, restricting access to specific ports, protocols, and IP addresses based on security policies and compliance requirements. Another technique for isolating virtual machines is to use hypervisor-based security features such as virtualization-based security (VBS) or secure enclaves, which provide hardware-level isolation and protection for sensitive workloads and data within virtualized environments. VBS leverages hardware-based security features such as Intel Virtualization Technology for Directed I/O (VT-d) and Trusted Execution Technology (TXT) to create isolated execution environments called virtual secure mode (VSM), where sensitive processes and data can run securely without being accessed or tampered with by other VMs or the hypervisor itself. To enable VBS, organizations can use hypervisor-specific commands or tools to enable VBS features and configure virtual secure mode (VSM) settings, ensuring that sensitive workloads and data are protected from unauthorized access or interference. Additionally, organizations can use secure enclaves such as Intel Software Guard Extensions (SGX) or AMD Secure Encrypted Virtualization (SEV) to create encrypted memory regions within VMs, where sensitive data can be stored and processed securely without being accessed or compromised by other VMs or the hypervisor. In summary, Virtual Machine Isolation Techniques are essential for ensuring the security and integrity of virtualized environments by preventing unauthorized access or interference between VMs and protecting against potential security threats and attacks. By leveraging hardware-assisted virtualization, software-based isolation mechanisms, network segmentation, and hypervisor-based security features, organizations can create secure and resilient virtualized infrastructures that meet their business requirements and regulatory compliance obligations.

Container Image Security Scanning is a crucial aspect of ensuring the security and integrity of containerized applications by detecting and mitigating security vulnerabilities, malware, and other potential threats within container images before they are deployed in production environments. One popular tool for container image security scanning is Docker Security Scanning, which allows users to scan Docker container images for known security vulnerabilities, misconfigurations, and compliance issues using automated vulnerability detection techniques and curated vulnerability databases. To perform a security scan using Docker Security Scanning, users can use the docker scan command followed by the name of the Docker image they want to scan, such as docker scan my-image, which will initiate a scan of the specified Docker image and generate a report detailing any vulnerabilities or issues found. Additionally, Docker Security Scanning integrates with Docker Hub, allowing users to automatically scan Docker images as they are pushed to Docker Hub repositories and receive security scan results directly within the Docker Hub user interface. Another tool for container image security scanning is Clair, an open-source vulnerability scanner designed specifically for container images that integrates with container registries such as Docker Registry, Amazon ECR, and Google Container Registry. To perform a security scan using Clair, users can use the clairctl command-line tool to scan container images stored in a container registry, such as clairctl vulnerability report my-image, which will initiate a scan of the specified container image and generate a report detailing any vulnerabilities or issues found. Additionally, Clair integrates with container orchestration platforms such as Kubernetes and Docker Swarm, allowing users to automatically scan container images as they are deployed to production environments and receive security scan results within their existing workflow and toolchain. Another tool for container image security scanning is Anchore Engine, an open-source container analysis and policy enforcement platform that provides vulnerability scanning, compliance checking, and image signing capabilities for container images. To perform a security scan using Anchore Engine, users can use the anchore-cli command-line tool to analyze container images stored in a container registry, such as anchore-cli image add my-image, which will initiate a scan of the specified container image and add it to the Anchore Engine image analysis pipeline. Additionally, Anchore Engine integrates with continuous integration and continuous deployment (CI/CD) pipelines, allowing users to automatically scan container images as part of their build and release processes and enforce security policies and best practices throughout the software development lifecycle. Another tool for container image security scanning is Twistlock, a commercial container security platform that provides vulnerability management, runtime protection, and compliance enforcement capabilities for containerized applications. To perform a security scan using Twistlock, users can use the Twistlock console or API to scan container images stored in a container registry, such as twistcli images scan my-image, which will initiate a scan of the specified container image and generate a report detailing any vulnerabilities or issues found. Additionally, Twistlock integrates with container orchestration platforms such as Kubernetes and Docker Swarm, allowing users to automatically scan container images as they are deployed to production environments and enforce security policies and controls in real-time. In summary, Container Image Security Scanning is a critical process for ensuring the security and integrity of containerized applications by detecting and mitigating security vulnerabilities, malware, and other potential threats within container images before they are deployed in production environments. By leveraging tools such as Docker Security Scanning, Clair, Anchore Engine, and Twistlock, organizations can identify and remediate security issues early in the software development lifecycle, reduce the risk of security breaches and compliance violations, and maintain a strong security posture across their containerized infrastructure.

Container Runtime Security Controls are essential for protecting containerized applications against security threats and vulnerabilities during runtime, ensuring the confidentiality, integrity, and availability of sensitive data and resources within containerized environments. One fundamental aspect of container runtime security is controlling access to sensitive system resources and capabilities within containers, such as network interfaces, filesystems, and inter-process communication (IPC) mechanisms, to prevent unauthorized access or tampering by malicious actors. To enforce access controls and restrictions on system resources within containers, organizations can use Linux kernel security features such as namespaces, control groups (cgroups), and capabilities, which provide fine-grained isolation and control over containerized processes and resources. For example, organizations can use the docker run command with the --cap-drop flag to drop specific Linux capabilities from container processes, such as docker run --cap-drop=NET_RAW to prevent containers from creating raw network sockets and docker run --cap-drop=SYS_ADMIN to prevent containers from performing privileged system administration tasks. Additionally, organizations can use container runtime security tools such as SELinux (Security-Enhanced Linux) or AppArmor (Application Armor) to enforce mandatory access control (MAC) policies and restrict the actions that container processes can perform based on security labels and profiles. For example, organizations can use SELinux or AppArmor profiles to confine container processes to specific filesystem paths, limit network communication, and restrict access to sensitive system resources such as devices and kernel interfaces. Another aspect of container runtime security is protecting against container escape and privilege escalation attacks, where an attacker exploits vulnerabilities in container runtimes or host operating systems to gain unauthorized access to the underlying host system or other containers. To mitigate the risk of container escape and privilege escalation attacks, organizations should regularly update and patch container runtimes and host operating systems to address known security vulnerabilities and apply security best practices such as least privilege and principle of least privilege (PoLP) to limit the capabilities and permissions granted to containerized processes. Additionally, organizations can use container runtime security tools such as Docker Security Scanning, Clair, or Anchore Engine to scan container images for known vulnerabilities and configuration issues before they are deployed in production environments and enforce security policies and controls to prevent insecure container deployments. Another aspect of container runtime security is monitoring and logging container activities and events to detect and respond to security threats and incidents in real-time. Organizations can use container runtime security tools such as Falco, Sysdig Secure, or Aqua Security to monitor container activities and behaviors, analyze system calls and events, and generate alerts or notifications for suspicious or malicious behavior. For example, organizations can use Falco rules to detect unauthorized file access, network communication, or privilege escalation attempts within containers and trigger automated responses such as blocking network traffic, killing or restarting containers, or alerting security teams for further investigation. Additionally, organizations can integrate container runtime security tools with centralized logging and monitoring platforms such as Elasticsearch, Splunk, or Grafana to aggregate and analyze container logs and telemetry data, correlate security events across distributed environments, and generate comprehensive security reports and dashboards for compliance and audit purposes. In summary, Container Runtime Security

Controls are essential for protecting containerized applications against security threats and vulnerabilities during runtime by enforcing access controls and restrictions, protecting against container escape and privilege escalation attacks, and monitoring and logging container activities and events for detection and response. By implementing security best practices and leveraging container runtime security tools and technologies, organizations can build secure and resilient containerized infrastructures that meet their business requirements and regulatory compliance obligations.

Network Segmentation Strategies are fundamental to enhancing cybersecurity posture by partitioning networks into smaller, isolated segments to contain and mitigate the impact of security breaches and unauthorized access attempts. One effective approach to network segmentation is using virtual local area networks (VLANs), which allow organizations to logically divide a physical network into multiple virtual networks, each with its own broadcast domain and security policies. To configure VLANs, network administrators can use switches that support VLAN tagging and trunking protocols such as IEEE 802.1Q, which enable the tagging of Ethernet frames with VLAN identifiers to identify traffic belonging to different VLANs. By assigning VLAN memberships to switch ports and defining VLAN-specific access control policies, organizations can isolate and control network traffic between different VLANs, preventing unauthorized access and lateral movement within the network. Another network segmentation strategy is using subnetting to divide IP address ranges into smaller subnetworks based on specific criteria such as geographic location, departmental boundaries, or security requirements. To implement subnetting, organizations can use IP addressing schemes such as Classless Inter-Domain Routing (CIDR) notation to allocate IP address ranges to different subnetworks and define subnet masks to determine the size and scope of each subnet. By segmenting the network into smaller subnets, organizations can reduce the size of broadcast domains, improve network performance, and enforce access controls and security policies at the subnet level to restrict communication between different network segments. Additionally, organizations can use access control lists (ACLs) and firewall rules to filter and control traffic between different subnets, allowing or denying specific types of traffic based on source and destination IP addresses, port numbers, and protocols. Another network segmentation strategy is using software-defined networking (SDN) technologies to create virtual network overlays and microsegmentation policies that dynamically isolate and secure workloads and applications within cloud and data center environments. To implement microsegmentation using SDN, organizations can use software-defined networking controllers and orchestration platforms such as VMware NSX, Cisco Application Centric Infrastructure (ACI), or OpenStack Neutron to define granular network segmentation policies based on application attributes, user identities, or security labels. By enforcing microsegmentation policies at the network level, organizations can isolate and protect critical workloads and applications from lateral movement and unauthorized access attempts, reducing the attack surface and minimizing the impact of security breaches. Additionally, organizations can use network segmentation to enforce zero-trust networking principles by requiring authentication and authorization for every network communication, regardless of the source or destination. This approach helps prevent unauthorized access to sensitive resources and data by limiting network access based on user identities, device characteristics, and security posture assessments. By implementing network segmentation strategies and enforcing zero-trust networking principles, organizations can strengthen their cybersecurity defenses, improve visibility and control over network traffic, and reduce the risk of data breaches and compliance violations. Furthermore, organizations can use network segmentation to isolate and protect critical infrastructure and applications from malicious actors and insider threats, reducing the likelihood of successful cyber attacks and minimizing the impact of security incidents on business operations and continuity. In summary, Network Segmentation Strategies are essential for enhancing cybersecurity posture and mitigating the risk of security breaches and unauthorized access attempts by dividing networks into smaller, isolated segments and enforcing access controls and security policies to restrict communication between different network segments. By leveraging VLANs, subnetting, software-defined networking, and zero-trust networking principles, organizations can create secure and resilient network architectures that protect critical assets and data from cyber threats and vulnerabilities. Cloud Firewall Best Practices are essential for securing cloud-based infrastructures and protecting against unauthorized access, malicious activity, and data breaches. One key best practice is to deploy a cloud-native firewall solution, such as AWS Security Groups or Azure Network Security Groups, to control inbound and outbound traffic to and from cloud resources. These cloud-native firewall solutions allow organizations to define security rules and policies that specify which traffic is allowed or denied based on source and destination IP addresses, port numbers, and protocols. To configure security groups in AWS, organizations can use the AWS Management Console or AWS Command Line Interface (CLI) to create security group rules and apply them to EC2 instances, RDS databases, and other AWS resources. Similarly, in Azure, organizations can use the Azure portal or Azure CLI to create network security group (NSG) rules and associate them with Azure virtual machines, virtual networks, and subnets. By implementing cloud-native firewall solutions, organizations can enforce least privilege access controls and restrict network traffic to only necessary and trusted sources, reducing the attack surface and minimizing the risk of unauthorized access. Another best practice for cloud firewall management is to regularly review and update firewall rules to ensure they align with security policies and compliance requirements. This includes conducting periodic security audits and risk assessments to identify and remediate misconfigurations, unused rules, and overly permissive access controls that may expose cloud resources to security risks. To audit and review firewall rules, organizations can use cloud-native monitoring and logging tools such as AWS CloudTrail, Azure Monitor, or Google Cloud Audit Logging to track changes to security group and network security group configurations, monitor network traffic patterns, and generate security reports and alerts for suspicious or anomalous activity. Additionally, organizations can leverage third-party cloud security platforms and services such as Palo Alto Networks Prisma Cloud, Check Point CloudGuard, or Fortinet FortiGate Cloud to automate firewall rule management, perform continuous compliance monitoring, and enforce security policies across multi-cloud environments. These cloud security platforms provide centralized visibility and control over firewall configurations, streamline firewall rule management workflows, and help organizations identify and address security gaps and compliance violations in real-time. Another best practice for cloud firewall management is to implement network segmentation and microsegmentation to isolate and protect cloud workloads and applications from lateral movement and unauthorized access attempts. This involves dividing cloud networks into smaller, isolated segments or security zones based on workload characteristics, user identities, or sensitivity levels and applying granular firewall rules and access controls to each segment. To implement network segmentation and microsegmentation in the cloud, organizations can use cloud-native network virtualization technologies such as Amazon VPC peering, Azure Virtual Network (VNet) peering, or Google Cloud VPC peering to establish private communication channels between virtual networks and subnets within the same cloud provider or across different cloud providers. Additionally, organizations can use cloud-native firewall features such as AWS Security Group rules, Azure NSG rules, or Google Cloud firewall rules to enforce network segmentation and microsegmentation policies at the network level, restricting communication between different segments based on predefined security policies and access controls. By implementing network segmentation and microsegmentation, organizations can reduce the scope of potential security breaches, contain security incidents, and protect sensitive data and resources from unauthorized access and exfiltration. In summary, Cloud Firewall Best Practices are essential for securing cloud-based infrastructures and protecting against unauthorized access, malicious activity, and data breaches by deploying cloud-native firewall solutions, regularly reviewing and updating firewall rules, implementing network segmentation and microsegmentation, and leveraging third-party cloud security platforms and services. By following these best practices, organizations can establish strong and resilient cloud security postures that meet their business requirements and compliance obligations while minimizing the risk of security incidents and breaches.

Federated Identity Management plays a pivotal role in modern IT landscapes, facilitating seamless and secure access to resources across different domains, applications, and organizations. One prominent aspect of federated identity management is Single Sign-On (SSO), which allows users to access multiple applications and services with a single set of credentials, reducing the burden of managing multiple passwords and enhancing user experience. To implement SSO, organizations can deploy identity providers (IdPs) such as Microsoft Azure Active Directory, Okta, or Ping Identity, which authenticate users and issue security tokens that grant access to federated applications and services. These identity providers support industry-standard protocols such as Security Assertion Markup Language (SAML), OpenID Connect, and OAuth, which enable seamless authentication and authorization workflows between IdPs and service providers. By configuring federated trust relationships between identity providers and service providers, organizations can enable users to authenticate once with their IdP credentials and access federated applications and services without needing to re-enter their credentials. Another aspect of federated identity management is attribute-based access control (ABAC), which enables organizations to define access policies based on user attributes such as role, department, location, and device type, rather than relying solely on user identities. To implement ABAC, organizations can use identity and access management (IAM) platforms such as AWS IAM, Azure RBAC, or Google Cloud IAM, which provide fine-grained access control capabilities and support dynamic authorization based on user attributes and contextual information. These IAM platforms allow organizations to define access policies that grant or deny access to resources based on user attributes and environmental factors, ensuring that users have the appropriate level of access based on their roles and responsibilities. Additionally, organizations can leverage standards-based protocols such as XACML (eXtensible Access Control Markup Language) to define and enforce attribute-based access policies across federated environments. Another aspect of federated identity management is identity federation, which enables organizations to establish trust relationships between different identity providers and share user identities and authentication tokens across federated domains. To implement identity federation, organizations can use standards-based federation protocols such as SAML, OpenID Connect, or WS-Federation to establish trust relationships between IdPs and service providers, allowing users to authenticate with their home IdP credentials and access federated resources in partner domains. By federating identities across different domains and organizations, organizations can streamline user access and collaboration, reduce the overhead of managing separate user accounts and credentials, and improve security by centralizing identity management and authentication mechanisms. Additionally, organizations can use identity federation to enable seamless access to cloud-based applications and services, allowing users to authenticate with their corporate credentials and access federated resources in public cloud environments without needing to create separate accounts or credentials. Another aspect of federated identity management is identity brokering, which enables organizations to integrate multiple identity providers and authentication mechanisms into a single authentication flow, providing users with flexibility and choice in how they authenticate to federated applications and services. To implement identity brokering, organizations can use identity federation platforms such as Auth0, AWS Cognito, or Azure AD B2C, which provide centralized authentication and authorization capabilities and support integration with multiple identity providers and authentication protocols. These identity brokering platforms allow organizations to define authentication policies and workflows that accommodate different user authentication preferences and requirements, such as social login, multi-factor authentication (MFA), or passwordless authentication. By implementing identity brokering, organizations can provide users with a seamless and consistent authentication experience across federated applications and services, regardless of the underlying identity providers and authentication mechanisms. In summary, Federated Identity Management is a critical component of modern IT architectures, enabling seamless and secure access to resources across different domains, applications, and organizations by leveraging technologies such as Single Sign-On (SSO), attribute-based access control (ABAC), identity federation, and identity brokering. By adopting federated identity management practices, organizations can improve user experience, streamline access management, and enhance security posture in federated environments.

Attribute-Based Access Control (ABAC) is a dynamic and flexible access control model that allows organizations to make access control decisions based on attributes associated with users, resources, and environmental factors, rather than relying solely on user identities or roles. One fundamental aspect of ABAC is defining a set of attributes that describe users, resources, and contextual information relevant to access control decisions. These attributes can include user roles, department affiliations, job titles, location information, device characteristics, and time of access, among others. To define attributes, organizations can use identity and access management (IAM) platforms such as AWS IAM, Azure RBAC, or Google Cloud IAM, which provide *capabilities for defining custom user attributes and associating them with user identities. Additionally, organizations can leverage identity federation protocols such as SAML, OpenID Connect, or OAuth to federate user attributes from external identity providers and include them in access control decisions. Once attributes are defined, organizations can use access control policies to specify the conditions under which users are granted or denied access to resources based on their attribute values. These policies can be expressed using policy languages such as XACML (eXtensible Access Control Markup Language) or implemented using policy engines and enforcement points integrated into IAM platforms or application frameworks. For example, organizations can use AWS IAM policies to define access control policies that grant or deny access to AWS resources based on user attributes such as department, role, or team membership. Similarly, in Azure, organizations can use Azure RBAC policies to define role assignments and access scopes based on user attributes and resource properties. Another aspect of ABAC is evaluating access control policies dynamically at runtime based on the attributes and conditions present in access requests. This dynamic evaluation enables organizations to enforce fine-grained access control decisions tailored to specific contexts and scenarios. To evaluate access control policies dynamically, organizations can use policy decision points (PDPs) integrated into IAM platforms or application frameworks, which receive access requests and evaluate them against defined policies to determine whether access should be granted or denied. Additionally, organizations can use attribute-based access control frameworks and libraries such as AuthZForce or AuthZForce-PDP to implement dynamic policy evaluation and enforcement in custom applications and services. By dynamically evaluating access control policies based on attribute values and contextual information, organizations can enforce access controls that adapt to changing user roles, resource properties, and environmental factors, ensuring that access decisions remain relevant and effective over time. Another aspect of ABAC is enforcing access control policies consistently across different types of resources and access scenarios. This consistency enables organizations to apply a unified access control model across diverse IT environments, including cloud-based applications, on-premises systems, and hybrid infrastructures. To enforce access control policies consistently, organizations can use centralized policy management and enforcement points integrated into IAM platforms or application frameworks, which enforce access controls based on defined policies and attribute values. Additionally, organizations can use policy enforcement points (PEPs) deployed as gateways or intermediaries in application architectures to intercept access requests and enforce access control policies before granting access to protected resources. By enforcing access control policies consistently across different types of resources and access scenarios, organizations can reduce the complexity of access management, improve security posture, and ensure compliance with regulatory requirements and security standards. Another aspect of ABAC is integrating attribute-based access control with other access control models and mechanisms, such as role-based access control (RBAC) and mandatory access control (MAC), to provide layered defense and defense-in-depth security. This integration enables organizations to combine the strengths of different access control models and mechanisms to address diverse security requirements and use cases effectively. To integrate ABAC with other access control models and mechanisms, organizations can use IAM platforms and access management frameworks that support flexible policy composition and evaluation, allowing them to define complex access control policies that incorporate elements of ABAC, RBAC, and MAC. Additionally, organizations can use access control policy languages and standards such as XACML or NIST RBAC to express policies that combine attributes, roles, and permissions in a unified policy framework. By integrating attribute-based access control with other access control models and mechanisms, organizations can implement comprehensive access management strategies that provide granular control over access to resources, enforce least privilege principles, and mitigate the risk of unauthorized access and data breaches. In summary, Attribute-Based Access Control (ABAC) is a dynamic and flexible access control model that allows organizations to make access control decisions based on attributes associated with users, resources, and environmental factors. By defining attributes, implementing access control policies, dynamically evaluating policies, enforcing policies consistently, and integrating ABAC with other access control models and mechanisms, organizations can establish robust and adaptive access management strategies that meet their security requirements and compliance objectives effectively.*

Data Encryption in Transit and at Rest is a fundamental aspect of data security that aims to protect sensitive information from unauthorized access and interception while it is being transmitted between systems or stored on storage devices. One important technique for encrypting data in transit is using Secure Sockets Layer (SSL) or Transport Layer Security (TLS) protocols to establish secure communication channels between clients and servers over untrusted networks such as the internet. To enable SSL/TLS encryption for network communications, organizations can configure web servers such as Apache HTTP Server or Nginx to support SSL/TLS by generating and installing SSL/TLS certificates issued by trusted certificate authorities (CAs). Additionally, organizations can use SSL/TLS termination proxies or load balancers such as HAProxy or AWS Elastic Load Balancing (ELB) to offload SSL/TLS encryption and decryption from backend servers, improving performance and scalability while maintaining end-to-end encryption between clients and servers. By encrypting data in transit using SSL/TLS, organizations can protect sensitive information from eavesdropping, man-in-the-middle attacks, and data interception during network transmissions. Another technique for encrypting data in transit is using Virtual Private Network (VPN) technologies to create secure and encrypted tunnels between network endpoints, allowing remote users and branch offices to securely access corporate networks and resources over untrusted networks such as the internet. To deploy a VPN, organizations can use VPN software or appliances such as OpenVPN, Cisco AnyConnect, or Palo Alto Networks GlobalProtect to establish encrypted connections between client devices and VPN gateways or concentrators deployed in corporate data centers or cloud environments. Additionally, organizations can use VPN protocols such as IPsec (Internet Protocol Security) or SSL VPN to encrypt network traffic and authenticate users before allowing them to access internal resources and applications. By encrypting data in transit using VPN technologies, organizations can ensure the confidentiality and integrity of network communications, even when traversing untrusted or public networks. Another important aspect of data encryption is encrypting data at rest, which involves encrypting sensitive data before storing it on storage devices such as hard disk drives (HDDs), solid-state drives (SSDs), or cloud storage services to protect it from unauthorized access and disclosure. One common approach to encrypting data at rest is using full disk encryption (FDE) or file-level encryption (FLE) technologies to encrypt entire storage volumes or individual files and folders. To implement full disk encryption, organizations can use operating system features such as BitLocker on Windows or FileVault on macOS to encrypt entire hard drives or partitions using symmetric encryption algorithms such as AES (Advanced Encryption Standard). Additionally, organizations can use third-party encryption software such as VeraCrypt or Symantec Endpoint Encryption to encrypt storage volumes on servers, workstations, and mobile devices to protect sensitive data from unauthorized access and theft. By encrypting data at rest using full disk encryption or file-level encryption, organizations can ensure that sensitive information remains protected even if storage devices are lost, stolen, or accessed by unauthorized individuals. Another technique for encrypting data at rest is using database encryption technologies to encrypt sensitive data stored in databases such as Oracle, SQL Server, or MySQL to protect it from unauthorized access and disclosure. To implement database encryption, organizations can use database management system (DBMS) features such as Transparent Data Encryption (TDE) or column-level encryption to encrypt database tables, columns, or individual data elements using encryption keys managed by the DBMS. Additionally, organizations can use hardware security modules (HSMs) or key management services (KMSs) to store and manage encryption keys securely, ensuring that only authorized users and applications can access encrypted data. By encrypting data at rest using database encryption technologies, organizations can mitigate the risk of data breaches and comply with regulatory requirements and industry standards such as the Payment Card Industry Data Security Standard (PCI DSS) or the Health Insurance Portability and Accountability Act (HIPAA). In summary, Data Encryption in Transit and at Rest is a critical aspect of data security that helps organizations protect sensitive information from unauthorized access and interception while it is being transmitted between systems or stored on storage devices. By encrypting data in transit using SSL/TLS or VPN technologies and encrypting data at rest using full disk encryption or database encryption, organizations can ensure the confidentiality, integrity, and availability of sensitive data, even in the face of evolving security threats and vulnerabilities.

Key Rotation and Key Escrow are critical aspects of cryptographic key management that ensure the security and integrity of encrypted data over time. Key Rotation involves regularly replacing cryptographic keys with new ones to minimize the risk of key compromise and to align with security best practices and compliance requirements. One common approach to key rotation is to generate new encryption keys at regular intervals using automated processes or cryptographic algorithms such as AES (Advanced Encryption Standard) or RSA (Rivest–Shamir–Adleman) and then update encryption configurations to use the new keys. For example, in AWS Key Management Service (KMS), organizations can use the AWS Management Console or AWS CLI (Command Line Interface) to rotate customer master keys (CMKs) using the aws kms enable-key-rotation command to enable automatic key rotation and the aws kms rotate-key command to manually rotate keys. Similarly, in Azure Key Vault, organizations can use the Azure portal or Azure CLI to enable key rotation for keys stored in key vaults using the az keyvault rotation-policy update command to configure key rotation policies and the az keyvault key rotate command to manually rotate keys. By regularly rotating encryption keys, organizations can reduce the likelihood of unauthorized access to encrypted data and mitigate the impact of key compromise or exposure. Another aspect of key rotation is managing the rotation process to ensure minimal disruption to operations and to maintain data availability and accessibility. This includes defining key rotation schedules and policies based on security requirements and risk assessments and *implementing automated key rotation mechanisms to streamline the process and minimize manual intervention. Additionally, organizations should consider implementing key rotation notifications and logging to track key rotation activities and to identify any issues or anomalies that may arise during the process. By effectively managing key rotation, organizations can maintain the security and integrity of encrypted data while minimizing the impact on operational workflows and user experience. Key Escrow is the process of securely storing and managing cryptographic keys by trusted third parties or escrow agents to ensure their availability and recoverability in case of key loss, damage, or compromise. Escrowed keys are typically stored in secure and tamper-evident environments such as hardware security modules (HSMs) or dedicated key management systems (KMSs) and are protected using strong encryption and access controls to prevent unauthorized access or disclosure. One common use case for key escrow is in enterprise encryption systems where organizations need to ensure access to encrypted data even if the original encryption keys are lost or unavailable. For example, in the event of a hardware failure or a key management error, organizations can retrieve escrowed keys from trusted escrow agents to recover encrypted data and resume operations. In addition to data recovery, key escrow is also used in regulatory compliance and law enforcement scenarios where access to encrypted data may be required for legal or investigatory purposes. For example, organizations subject to regulatory requirements such as the Health Insurance Portability and Accountability Act (HIPAA) or the European Union's General Data Protection Regulation (GDPR) may be required to maintain escrowed keys to comply with data access and disclosure mandates. Similarly, law enforcement agencies may request access to escrowed keys as part of criminal investigations or court orders to decrypt and access encrypted data. By implementing key escrow mechanisms, organizations can ensure the availability and recoverability of cryptographic keys and maintain compliance with regulatory requirements and legal obligations. However, it's important to note that key escrow introduces additional security and privacy risks, as escrowed keys may become targets for unauthorized access or misuse. Therefore, organizations should implement robust security controls and access management policies to protect escrowed keys and minimize the risk of unauthorized disclosure or misuse. Additionally, organizations should regularly audit and monitor key escrow activities to detect and respond to any security incidents or policy violations. In summary, Key Rotation and Key Escrow are essential components of cryptographic key management that help organizations maintain the security and integrity of encrypted data over time. By regularly rotating encryption keys and implementing key escrow mechanisms, organizations can minimize the risk of key compromise, ensure the availability and recoverability of cryptographic keys, and comply with regulatory requirements and legal obligations.*

Cloud Security Policy Automation is a crucial aspect of managing and enforcing security policies in cloud environments, allowing organizations to streamline security operations, enhance compliance, and mitigate security risks. One primary objective of policy automation is to automate the enforcement of security policies across cloud services and resources to ensure consistent and scalable security controls. Organizations can achieve this by leveraging Infrastructure as Code (IaC) tools such as Terraform, AWS CloudFormation, or Azure Resource Manager (ARM) templates to define security policies as code and deploy them automatically alongside cloud resources. For instance, in Terraform, organizations can use the terraform plan and terraform apply commands to preview and apply changes to infrastructure configurations defined in Terraform scripts, including security policies such as access control rules, encryption settings, and compliance checks. Similarly, in AWS CloudFormation, organizations can use CloudFormation templates to define security policies and resource configurations and deploy them using the aws cloudformation deploy command or through the AWS Management Console. By automating security policy enforcement through IaC tools, organizations can reduce the risk of misconfigurations, ensure compliance with security standards and best practices, and accelerate the deployment of secure cloud infrastructure. Another key aspect of cloud security policy automation is the continuous monitoring and enforcement of security policies to detect and remediate security issues in real-time. This involves implementing automated monitoring and alerting mechanisms that notify security teams of policy violations or deviations from desired security configurations. Organizations can use cloud-native monitoring and logging services such as AWS CloudTrail, Azure Monitor, or Google Cloud Audit Logging to capture and analyze security-related events and activities across cloud environments. Additionally, organizations can use Security Information and Event Management (SIEM) platforms such as Splunk, Elastic SIEM, or IBM QRadar to aggregate and correlate security events from multiple cloud services and resources, enabling proactive threat detection and incident response. By integrating monitoring and alerting capabilities with security policy automation frameworks, organizations can enforce security policies dynamically, respond to security incidents promptly, and maintain continuous compliance with regulatory requirements and security standards. Furthermore, cloud security policy automation facilitates the integration of security into the DevOps pipeline, enabling organizations to embed security controls and compliance checks into the software development lifecycle (SDLC) and continuous integration/continuous deployment (CI/CD) workflows. This involves integrating security scanning tools, vulnerability assessments, and compliance checks into CI/CD pipelines to automate security testing and validation of cloud-native applications and infrastructure. For example, organizations can use DevSecOps tools such as HashiCorp Vault, Snyk, or Twistlock to automate security scanning and vulnerability assessments of container images, serverless functions, or Kubernetes configurations as part of the CI/CD process. By automating security policy enforcement in the DevOps pipeline, organizations can identify and remediate security issues early in the development lifecycle, minimize security risks, and accelerate the delivery of secure and compliant cloud applications. Additionally, cloud security policy automation enables organizations to achieve governance and compliance objectives by implementing automated policy enforcement and reporting mechanisms that demonstrate adherence to internal policies, industry regulations, and contractual obligations. Organizations can use policy-based compliance frameworks such as the Center for Internet Security (CIS) benchmarks, NIST Special Publication 800-53, or the Payment Card Industry Data Security Standard (PCI DSS) to define security baselines and automate compliance checks across cloud environments. For instance, organizations can use AWS Config rules, Azure Policy, or Google Cloud Security Command Center (SCC) to define and enforce *custom compliance policies and automatically remediate non-compliant resources using predefined actions or remediation scripts. By automating governance and compliance processes, organizations can reduce manual effort, minimize human error, and demonstrate continuous compliance with regulatory requirements and industry standards. In summary, Cloud Security Policy Automation is essential for managing and enforcing security policies effectively in cloud environments, enabling organizations to automate security controls, enhance compliance, and mitigate security risks. By leveraging Infrastructure as Code (IaC) tools, continuous monitoring and enforcement mechanisms, integration with DevOps practices, and automated governance and compliance frameworks, organizations can establish a robust and scalable security posture that aligns with business objectives and regulatory requirements in the cloud. Automated Incident Response Workflows play a crucial role in modern cybersecurity operations, enabling organizations to detect, investigate, and mitigate security incidents rapidly and efficiently. These workflows automate key incident response tasks and orchestrate the response process across people, processes, and technologies to minimize the impact of security breaches and protect organizational assets. One essential component of automated incident response workflows is the integration of security orchestration, automation, and response (SOAR) platforms, which provide a centralized framework for designing, executing, and managing incident response processes. Organizations can use SOAR platforms such as Demisto, Splunk Phantom, or IBM Resilient to create incident response playbooks that define the sequence of actions to be taken in response to specific types of security incidents. For example, organizations can define playbooks to automatically triage alerts, gather additional context from security tools and threat intelligence sources, and orchestrate response actions such as blocking malicious IP addresses, quarantining infected hosts, or resetting compromised user accounts. By integrating SOAR platforms with security tools and systems using APIs (Application Programming Interfaces) or integrations, organizations can streamline incident response workflows and accelerate response times while reducing manual effort and human error. Another aspect of automated incident response workflows is the use of security automation and orchestration (SAO) scripts or scripts to automate repetitive and time-consuming tasks during incident response. Organizations can use scripting languages such as Python, PowerShell, or Bash to develop custom automation scripts that perform specific incident response actions, such as querying log data, analyzing malware samples, or remediating security vulnerabilities. For example, organizations can use PowerShell scripts to remotely disable compromised user accounts or terminate malicious processes on infected endpoints, or they can use Python scripts to parse and analyze network traffic logs for signs of suspicious activity. By leveraging automation scripts, organizations can accelerate incident response processes, improve consistency and repeatability, and free up security analysts to focus on more complex tasks that require human judgment and expertise. Additionally, automated incident response workflows often incorporate machine learning and artificial intelligence (AI) techniques to enhance threat detection and response capabilities. Organizations can use machine learning algorithms to analyze large volumes of security data and identify patterns, anomalies, and indicators of compromise (IOCs) that may indicate a security incident. For example, organizations can use supervised machine learning models to classify security alerts based on historical incident data and prioritize alerts for further investigation and response. Similarly, organizations can use unsupervised machine learning techniques such as clustering or anomaly detection to identify deviations from normal behavior and detect unknown or emerging threats. By integrating machine learning capabilities into automated incident response workflows, organizations can improve the accuracy and efficiency of threat detection, reduce false positives, and respond to security incidents more effectively. Moreover, automated incident response workflows often leverage threat intelligence feeds and external data sources to enrich security alerts and provide additional context for incident investigation and response. Organizations can subscribe to threat intelligence services such as ISACs (Information Sharing and Analysis Centers), commercial threat intelligence providers, or open-source threat feeds to access up-to-date information about known threats, vulnerabilities, and adversary tactics, techniques, and procedures (TTPs). For example, organizations can integrate threat intelligence feeds into their SIEM (Security Information and Event Management) systems or SOAR platforms to automatically correlate security events with known indicators of compromise (IOCs) and prioritize incident response efforts based on the severity and relevance of threats. By incorporating threat intelligence into automated incident response workflows, organizations can enhance their ability to detect and respond to advanced threats, proactively identify potential security risks, and make more informed decisions about incident prioritization and resource allocation. Additionally, automated incident response workflows often include post-incident analysis and reporting capabilities to assess the effectiveness of incident response efforts and identify opportunities for improvement. Organizations can use data analytics and visualization tools to analyze incident response metrics such as mean time to detect (MTTD), mean time to respond (MTTR), and mean time to recover (MTTR) to measure the efficiency and effectiveness of their incident response processes. For example, organizations can use dashboards and reports to track key performance indicators (KPIs) related to incident response, such as the number of security incidents detected and resolved, the average response times for different types of incidents, and the impact of incidents on business operations. By analyzing incident response metrics and trends, organizations can identify bottlenecks, gaps, and areas for optimization in their incident response workflows and implement corrective actions to improve their overall security posture and resilience to cyber threats. In summary, Automated Incident Response Workflows are essential for organizations to detect, investigate, and mitigate security incidents rapidly and effectively in today's complex and dynamic threat landscape. By integrating SOAR platforms, automation scripts, machine learning algorithms, threat intelligence feeds, and post-incident analysis capabilities into their incident response workflows, organizations can streamline their response processes, improve threat detection and response capabilities, and enhance their overall security posture.*

Real-time Log Analysis and Monitoring is a critical component of modern cybersecurity and IT operations, enabling organizations to detect and respond to security threats, performance issues, and operational anomalies as they occur. By continuously monitoring logs generated by systems, applications, network devices, and cloud services in real-time, organizations can gain valuable insights into their IT environments, identify suspicious activities or events, and take immediate action to mitigate risks and ensure the integrity and availability of their systems and data. One key aspect of real-time log analysis and monitoring is the collection and aggregation of log data from various sources across the IT infrastructure. Organizations can use centralized logging solutions such as Elasticsearch, Logstash, and Kibana (ELK stack), Splunk, or Sumo Logic to collect, parse, index, and analyze log data from diverse sources in real-time. For example, in the ELK stack, organizations can use Logstash to collect log data from different sources using input plugins such as Filebeat for log files, Metricbeat for system metrics, and Packetbeat for network traffic, and then index the data into Elasticsearch for storage and search. They can then use Kibana to visualize and analyze log data through interactive dashboards and visualizations. By centralizing log data in a unified platform, organizations can correlate events across different systems and applications, identify patterns and trends, and detect anomalies or security incidents more effectively. Another aspect of real-time log analysis and monitoring is the use of alerting and notification mechanisms to notify IT and security teams of critical events or anomalies as they occur. Organizations can configure alerting rules based on predefined thresholds, patterns, or signatures to trigger notifications when specific conditions are met. For example, in the ELK stack, organizations can use Watcher, a feature of Elasticsearch, to define alerting rules that monitor log data in real-time and trigger actions such as sending email alerts, executing custom scripts, or integrating with third-party incident response platforms like PagerDuty or Slack. Similarly, in Splunk, organizations can use the Splunk Alert Manager to create alerting policies that generate notifications based on search queries or predefined conditions in log data. By implementing proactive alerting and notification mechanisms, organizations can respond to security incidents and operational issues promptly, minimize the impact of disruptions, and maintain the resilience and availability of their IT infrastructure. Additionally, real-time log analysis and monitoring enable organizations to perform proactive threat hunting and incident investigation activities to identify and respond to emerging threats and security risks before they escalate. Security teams can use advanced analytics and search capabilities to search, filter, and analyze log data for indicators of compromise (IOCs), abnormal behaviors, or patterns associated with known attack techniques. For example, organizations can use query languages such as Elasticsearch Query DSL or Splunk SPL (Search Processing Language) to construct complex search queries that filter log data based on specific criteria, such as IP addresses, user agents, or event types, and then analyze the results to identify potential security threats. By proactively hunting for threats in real-time log data, organizations can detect and mitigate security incidents more effectively, reduce dwell time, and prevent potential data breaches or system compromises. Furthermore, real-time log analysis and monitoring facilitate compliance with regulatory requirements and industry standards by providing organizations with the visibility and auditability needed to demonstrate compliance with security policies and data protection regulations. Organizations can use logging solutions to capture and retain log data for audit and forensic purposes, generate compliance reports, and monitor adherence to security controls and best practices. For example, in the ELK stack, organizations can use the Security and Compliance app for Kibana to visualize and analyze log data for compliance with security standards such as PCI DSS, HIPAA, or GDPR, and generate compliance reports that document their compliance posture. Similarly, in Splunk, organizations can use the Splunk

App for PCI Compliance to monitor and report on PCI DSS compliance requirements using predefined dashboards and reports. By leveraging real-time log analysis and monitoring for compliance purposes, organizations can streamline audit processes, reduce compliance-related costs and efforts, and demonstrate their commitment to protecting sensitive data and maintaining regulatory compliance. In summary, Real-time Log Analysis and Monitoring are essential for organizations to detect and respond to security threats, performance issues, and operational anomalies in real-time, enabling them to maintain the integrity, availability, and resilience of their IT infrastructure. By centralizing log data, implementing proactive alerting mechanisms, conducting proactive threat hunting activities, and facilitating compliance with regulatory requirements, organizations can strengthen their security posture, improve incident response capabilities, and mitigate the risks associated with cyber threats and data breaches. Cloud Security Metrics and Key Performance Indicators (KPIs) are essential tools for organizations to measure, track, and improve the effectiveness of their cloud security programs, enabling them to assess their security posture, identify areas for improvement, and demonstrate the value of their security investments. These metrics and KPIs provide organizations with quantitative and qualitative insights into various aspects of cloud security, including risk management, threat detection and response, compliance, and operational efficiency. One key metric in cloud security is the Mean Time to Detect (MTTD), which measures the average time it takes for organizations to detect security incidents or anomalies in their cloud environments. Organizations can calculate MTTD by dividing the total time taken to detect security incidents by the number of incidents detected during a specific period. For example, organizations can use security monitoring tools such as AWS CloudTrail, Azure Monitor, or Google Cloud Audit Logging to capture and analyze security events in real-time and calculate the MTTD using the following formula: MTTD = Total time taken to detect security incidents / Number of security incidents detected. By monitoring MTTD over time, organizations can assess the effectiveness of their security monitoring capabilities, identify trends and patterns in security incidents, and implement measures to reduce detection times and enhance threat visibility. Another important metric in cloud security is the Mean Time to Respond (MTTR), which measures the average time it takes for organizations to respond to security incidents or breaches once they have been detected. Organizations can calculate MTTR by dividing the total time taken to respond to security incidents by the number of incidents responded to during a specific period. For example, organizations can use incident response platforms such as Demisto, Splunk Phantom, or IBM Resilient to automate and orchestrate incident response processes and calculate the MTTR using the following formula: MTTR = Total time taken to respond to security incidents / Number of security incidents responded to. By monitoring MTTR over time, organizations can assess the efficiency of their incident response processes, identify bottlenecks and inefficiencies, and implement measures to streamline response workflows and reduce response times. Additionally, organizations can track metrics related to cloud security controls and configurations to ensure compliance with security best practices and industry standards. For example, organizations can monitor the percentage of cloud resources with encryption enabled, the percentage of resources with proper access controls configured, or the number of misconfigured security groups or firewall rules. By monitoring these metrics, organizations can identify gaps in their security posture, prioritize remediation efforts, and ensure that their cloud environments adhere to security policies and compliance requirements. Furthermore, organizations can track metrics related to security incidents and breaches to assess the impact of security incidents on their business operations and reputation. For example, organizations can monitor the number of security incidents detected, the severity and impact of incidents, the cost of incident response and remediation efforts, and the time taken to recover from incidents. By analyzing these metrics, organizations can quantify the financial and reputational risks associated with security incidents, identify areas for improvement in their incident response processes, and allocate resources more effectively to mitigate future risks. Additionally, organizations can track metrics related to employee awareness and training to assess the effectiveness of their security awareness programs and ensure that employees are equipped with the knowledge and skills needed to protect against security threats. For example, organizations can monitor the completion rates of security awareness training courses, the results of phishing simulation exercises, or the number of security incidents caused by human error. By tracking these metrics, organizations can identify gaps in employee security awareness, tailor training programs to address specific needs, and reinforce a culture of security throughout the organization. In summary, Cloud Security Metrics and KPIs are essential for organizations to assess and improve their security posture in the cloud, enabling them to measure the effectiveness of their security programs, identify areas for improvement, and demonstrate the value of their security investments. By tracking metrics related to threat detection and response, security controls and configurations, incident impact and recovery, and employee awareness and training, organizations can make informed decisions to enhance their security posture and mitigate risks in the cloud.

Cloud Forensics Techniques are crucial for investigating security incidents, breaches, and unauthorized activities in cloud environments, enabling organizations to gather evidence, identify perpetrators, and mitigate risks effectively. These techniques encompass a range of methodologies, tools, and procedures tailored to the unique characteristics of cloud computing, including dynamic resource provisioning, shared responsibility models, and multi-tenant architectures. One fundamental aspect of cloud forensics is the collection and preservation of digital evidence from cloud-based systems, services, and applications. Organizations can use a variety of techniques to capture and retain relevant data for forensic analysis, including forensic imaging, live response, and memory forensics. For example, in Amazon Web Services (AWS), organizations can use the AWS CloudTrail service to capture API calls and log data from AWS services, which can then be stored in Amazon Simple Storage Service (S3) buckets for forensic analysis using tools like AWS Config or AWS CloudWatch Logs. Similarly, in Microsoft Azure, organizations can enable Azure Activity Logs and

Azure Security Center to capture audit logs and security events from Azure resources, which can be exported to Azure Storage or Azure Log Analytics for forensic analysis. By leveraging these cloud-native logging and monitoring capabilities, organizations can capture a comprehensive record of activities and events in their cloud environments, facilitating forensic investigations and incident response activities. Another critical aspect of cloud forensics is the analysis and interpretation of digital evidence to reconstruct events, identify root causes, and attribute responsibility for security incidents. Organizations can use forensic analysis techniques such as timeline analysis, file system analysis, and network traffic analysis to examine digital artifacts and uncover evidence of malicious activities or unauthorized access. For example, in Google Cloud Platform (GCP), organizations can use Google Cloud Logging and Google Cloud Monitoring to collect and analyze logs and metrics from GCP services, while also leveraging tools like Google Cloud Security Command Center (Cloud SCC) for threat detection and investigation. Similarly, organizations can use third-party forensic tools such as EnCase Forensic or Magnet AXIOM to analyze disk images, memory dumps, and network captures from cloud instances and virtual machines. By applying forensic analysis techniques to cloud-based evidence, organizations can reconstruct the sequence of events leading up to a security incident, identify compromised resources, and gather information necessary for remediation and legal proceedings. Additionally, cloud forensics techniques include chain of custody management, evidence authentication, and legal compliance to ensure that digital evidence is admissible in court and withstands legal scrutiny. Organizations must adhere to strict protocols for handling and preserving digital evidence, including documenting the chain of custody, maintaining integrity and confidentiality, and following established forensic best practices and standards. For example, organizations can use cryptographic hashes such as SHA-256 to calculate checksums for forensic images and log files, ensuring that data integrity is preserved throughout the investigation process. Moreover, organizations must comply with legal and regulatory requirements related to data privacy, confidentiality, and disclosure when conducting cloud forensics investigations. For example, organizations operating in regulated industries such as healthcare or finance must adhere to industry-specific regulations such as the Health Insurance Portability and Accountability Act (HIPAA) or the Payment Card Industry Data Security Standard (PCI DSS) when handling sensitive data or conducting forensic investigations. By integrating legal and regulatory compliance into their cloud forensics processes, organizations can mitigate legal risks, protect individual privacy rights, and ensure the admissibility of digital evidence in legal proceedings. In summary, Cloud Forensics Techniques are essential for organizations to investigate and respond to security incidents and breaches in cloud environments effectively. By leveraging cloud-native logging and monitoring capabilities, forensic analysis techniques, chain of custody management, and legal compliance measures, organizations can gather evidence, identify perpetrators, and mitigate risks in a timely and efficient manner. Threat Hunting in Cloud Environments is a proactive cybersecurity approach aimed at identifying and mitigating potential threats and security vulnerabilities before they can cause harm to an organization's cloud infrastructure, applications, or data. Unlike traditional security practices that primarily focus on reactive incident response, threat hunting involves actively searching for signs of malicious activity or suspicious behavior within cloud environments to detect and neutralize threats at an early stage. One fundamental aspect of threat hunting in cloud environments is the use of advanced analytics and machine learning techniques to analyze large volumes of data generated by cloud services, applications, and user activities. Organizations can leverage cloud-native security tools such as AWS GuardDuty, Azure

Sentinel, or Google Cloud Security Command Center (Cloud SCC) to collect and analyze logs, telemetry data, and network traffic in real-time, enabling security teams to identify anomalies, patterns, and indicators of compromise indicative of potential security threats. For example, security analysts can use query languages such as Amazon KQL (Kusto Query Language), Azure Log Analytics Query Language, or Google Cloud's BigQuery SQL to construct complex search queries that filter and analyze log data for suspicious activities, unauthorized access attempts, or anomalous behavior patterns. By applying advanced analytics and machine learning algorithms to cloud telemetry data, organizations can uncover hidden threats and security risks that may evade traditional security controls, enabling them to take proactive measures to mitigate risks and strengthen their security posture. Another essential aspect of threat hunting in cloud environments is the use of threat intelligence feeds and indicators of compromise (IOCs) to enrich security monitoring and detection capabilities. Organizations can subscribe to threat intelligence services such as AWS Security Hub, Azure Security Center, or Google Cloud Threat Intelligence to access curated threat feeds, malware signatures, and IOCs that can be used to identify known threats and suspicious activities in cloud environments. For example, security analysts can use the AWS Security Hub Findings API, Azure Security Center Alerts API, or Google Cloud Security Command Center API to programmatically retrieve threat intelligence data and enrich security alerts and findings with additional context and insights. By integrating threat intelligence into their threat hunting processes, organizations can enhance their ability to detect and respond to emerging threats, zero-day attacks, and advanced persistent threats (APTs) in cloud environments, enabling them to stay ahead of cyber adversaries and protect their critical assets and data. Additionally, threat hunting in cloud environments involves collaboration and knowledge sharing among security teams, cloud architects, and DevOps engineers to leverage their expertise and domain knowledge effectively. Organizations can establish cross-functional threat hunting teams comprising security analysts, cloud engineers, threat researchers, and incident responders to collaboratively investigate security incidents, share threat intelligence, and develop proactive mitigation strategies. For example, organizations can conduct regular threat hunting exercises and tabletop simulations to test their incident response procedures, validate security controls, and identify gaps in their security posture. By fostering a culture of collaboration and continuous learning, organizations can enhance their ability to detect and respond to evolving threats and security challenges in cloud environments, enabling them to adapt and evolve their security strategies to address emerging threats effectively. In summary, Threat Hunting in Cloud Environments is a proactive cybersecurity approach that enables organizations to detect and mitigate potential threats and security vulnerabilities before they can cause harm to their cloud infrastructure, applications, or data. By leveraging advanced analytics, threat intelligence, and cross-functional collaboration, organizations can uncover hidden threats, identify security risks, and strengthen their security posture in the cloud, enabling them to protect their critical assets and data from cyber adversaries.

Cloud Security Policy Frameworks are essential components of an organization's cybersecurity strategy, providing a structured approach to defining, implementing, and enforcing security policies and controls in cloud environments. These frameworks outline a set of rules, guidelines, and best practices designed to protect cloud resources, applications, and data from unauthorized access, misuse, and security threats. One widely used Cloud Security Policy Framework is the Cloud Security Alliance (CSA) Cloud Controls Matrix (CCM), which provides a comprehensive set of security controls mapped to leading cloud computing standards, regulations, and best practices. Organizations can use the CSA CCM to assess their cloud security posture, identify gaps in their security controls, and establish a baseline for implementing and monitoring security policies in the cloud. For example, organizations can use the CSA CCM to define security policies related to data encryption, access control, logging and monitoring, and incident response, ensuring compliance with industry standards such as ISO 27001, NIST SP 800-53, and GDPR. Another widely adopted Cloud Security Policy Framework is the Center for Internet Security (CIS) Benchmarks, which provides prescriptive guidance and best practices for securing various cloud platforms and services. Organizations can use the CIS Benchmarks to configure cloud resources, applications, and services according to industry-recognized security standards and guidelines, reducing the risk of security breaches and compliance violations. For example, organizations can use the CIS Benchmarks for AWS, Azure, and Google Cloud Platform (GCP) to configure security settings such as network access controls, identity and access management (IAM) policies, encryption settings, and logging and monitoring configurations, ensuring that their cloud environments adhere to industry best practices and security standards. Additionally, organizations can leverage industry-specific Cloud Security Policy Frameworks tailored to their unique regulatory and compliance requirements. For example, organizations operating in highly regulated industries such as healthcare, finance, or government can use frameworks such as the Health Information Trust Alliance (HITRUST) Common Security Framework (CSF), the Payment Card Industry Data Security Standard (PCI DSS), or the Federal Risk and Authorization Management Program (FedRAMP) to establish security policies and controls specific to their industry verticals. These frameworks provide detailed guidance and requirements for protecting sensitive data, ensuring data privacy and confidentiality, and meeting regulatory compliance obligations in cloud environments. Furthermore, organizations can develop custom Cloud Security Policy Frameworks tailored to their specific business needs, risk tolerance, and security objectives. These custom frameworks enable organizations to define security policies and controls that align with their unique business processes, applications, and risk factors, ensuring that their cloud security strategy is aligned with their overall business strategy. For example, organizations can develop custom security policies and controls for cloud-native applications, microservices architectures, or serverless computing environments, addressing emerging security challenges and leveraging cloud-native security capabilities such as containerization, orchestration, and serverless computing. In summary, Cloud Security Policy Frameworks are essential tools for organizations to define, implement, and enforce security policies and controls in cloud environments effectively. By leveraging industry-standard frameworks such as the CSA CCM, CIS Benchmarks, and industry-specific frameworks, organizations can establish a robust security posture, mitigate risks, and ensure compliance with regulatory requirements. Additionally, by developing custom Cloud Security Policy Frameworks tailored to their specific business needs, organizations can address unique security challenges, adapt to evolving threats, and protect their cloud resources, applications, and data from security breaches and cyber attacks.

Cloud Compliance Automation Solutions play a vital

role in streamlining and enhancing compliance management processes in cloud environments, enabling organizations to ensure adherence to regulatory requirements, industry standards, and internal policies. These solutions leverage automation technologies, including cloud-native tools, configuration management platforms, and policy enforcement mechanisms, to facilitate the continuous monitoring, assessment, and enforcement of compliance controls across cloud infrastructure, services, and applications. One key aspect of Cloud Compliance Automation Solutions is the use of infrastructure as code (IaC) and configuration management tools to enforce security and compliance policies through automated provisioning, configuration, and management of cloud resources. Organizations can use tools such as AWS CloudFormation, Azure Resource Manager (ARM) templates, or Google Cloud Deployment Manager to define infrastructure configurations as code, enabling them to automate the deployment of compliant cloud environments based on predefined security and compliance policies. For example, organizations can use AWS CloudFormation templates to define AWS resources such as Amazon EC2 instances, Amazon S3 buckets, and AWS IAM roles with built-in security controls and compliance checks, ensuring that cloud resources are provisioned securely and compliantly from the outset. Another important aspect of Cloud Compliance Automation Solutions is the integration of security and compliance checks into the continuous integration/continuous deployment (CI/CD) pipeline to enforce security and compliance requirements throughout the software development lifecycle. Organizations can use CI/CD platforms such as Jenkins, GitLab CI/CD, or AWS CodePipeline to automate the testing, validation, and deployment of code changes while also incorporating security and compliance checks into the pipeline. For example, organizations can use Jenkins pipeline scripts to perform static code analysis, vulnerability scanning, and compliance checks on application code before deploying it to production environments, ensuring that code changes adhere to security and compliance requirements. Additionally, Cloud Compliance Automation Solutions enable organizations to automate the collection, aggregation, and analysis of compliance data from disparate sources, including cloud logs, audit trails, and configuration files, to generate comprehensive compliance reports and audit trails. Organizations can use cloud-native logging and monitoring tools such as AWS CloudTrail, Azure Monitor, or Google Cloud Logging to capture and centralize audit logs and telemetry data from cloud services, applications, and infrastructure components, enabling them to monitor and track compliance-related activities in real-time. For example, organizations can use AWS Config Rules, Azure Policy, or Google Cloud Security Command Center (Cloud SCC) to define and enforce custom compliance rules and policies across their cloud environments, automatically flagging non-compliant resources and configurations for remediation. Moreover, Cloud Compliance Automation Solutions enable organizations to implement continuous compliance monitoring and enforcement capabilities, allowing them to detect and remediate compliance violations in near real-time. Organizations can use cloud-native compliance automation platforms such as AWS Security Hub, Azure Security Center, or Google Cloud Security Command Center (Cloud SCC) to continuously monitor cloud resources, services, and configurations for compliance deviations and security risks, generating alerts and notifications for potential issues. For example, organizations can use AWS Security Hub's automated security checks and compliance standards to assess the security posture of their AWS accounts and resources against industry benchmarks such as the Center for Internet Security (CIS) AWS Foundations Benchmark or the Payment Card Industry Data Security Standard (PCI DSS), automatically flagging non-compliant resources and configurations for remediation. In summary, Cloud Compliance Automation Solutions offer organizations a scalable and efficient approach to managing compliance requirements in cloud environments, enabling them to automate the provisioning, configuration, monitoring, and enforcement of security and compliance controls across their cloud infrastructure, services, and applications. By leveraging automation technologies, integrating security and compliance into the CI/CD pipeline, and implementing continuous compliance monitoring and enforcement capabilities, organizations can enhance their security posture, reduce compliance risks, and ensure adherence to regulatory requirements and industry standards in the cloud.

BOOK 3
RISK MANAGEMENT IN THE CLOUD
STRATEGIES FOR CCSP PROFESSIONALS

ROB BOTWRIGHT

The Cloud Security Threat Landscape presents a complex and evolving set of challenges for organizations as they adopt cloud computing technologies and migrate their workloads, data, and applications to cloud environments. One prominent threat in the Cloud Security Threat Landscape is the risk of data breaches and unauthorized access to sensitive information stored in cloud repositories and services. Attackers may exploit misconfigured cloud storage buckets, weak authentication mechanisms, or vulnerabilities in cloud applications to gain unauthorized access to sensitive data, leading to data theft, exposure, or manipulation. For example, attackers can use automated tools to scan the internet for publicly accessible cloud storage buckets with misconfigured permissions, allowing them to view, download, or modify sensitive data stored in these buckets without authentication. Another significant threat in the Cloud Security Threat Landscape is the risk of account hijacking and credential theft, where attackers compromise user accounts, credentials, or access tokens to gain unauthorized access to cloud resources and services. Attackers may use phishing attacks, social engineering tactics, or malware to steal user credentials or exploit weak authentication mechanisms to gain access to cloud accounts, enabling them to launch further attacks or exfiltrate sensitive data. For example, attackers can use phishing emails impersonating legitimate cloud service providers to trick users into disclosing their login credentials or granting access to their accounts, allowing attackers to compromise the accounts and perform unauthorized actions. Additionally, the Cloud Security Threat Landscape includes the risk of insider threats and malicious insiders who abuse their privileges and access rights to compromise cloud environments or steal sensitive data for personal gain or malicious purposes. Insider threats may include disgruntled employees, contractors, or partners who intentionally misuse their access privileges, exfiltrate confidential information, or sabotage cloud infrastructure and services, posing a significant risk to organizational security and data integrity. For example, an insider with privileged access to cloud resources may abuse their privileges to bypass security controls, delete critical data, or disrupt cloud services, causing financial losses and reputational damage to the organization. Furthermore, the Cloud Security Threat Landscape encompasses the risk of malware and malicious code targeting cloud infrastructure, applications, and data, posing a threat to the confidentiality, integrity, and availability of cloud resources and services. Attackers may use malware such as ransomware, cryptominers, or botnets to infect cloud instances, compromise data, or disrupt cloud operations, leading to service downtime, data loss, or financial harm. For example, attackers can use malware to exploit vulnerabilities in cloud-based web applications, inject malicious code, or install backdoors to gain persistent access to cloud environments and compromise sensitive data. Additionally, the Cloud Security Threat Landscape includes the risk of distributed denial-of-service (DDoS) attacks targeting cloud infrastructure and services, aiming to overwhelm cloud resources, networks, or applications with malicious traffic, causing service disruptions or outages. Attackers may use botnets, amplification techniques, or spoofed IP addresses to launch large-scale DDoS attacks against cloud service providers or organizations, disrupting their operations and impacting their ability to deliver services to users. For example, attackers can use DDoS attack tools such as hping, LOIC (Low Orbit Ion Cannon), or Xerxes to flood cloud infrastructure with malicious traffic, saturating network bandwidth and causing service degradation or downtime. Furthermore, the Cloud Security Threat Landscape encompasses the risk of supply chain attacks targeting cloud service providers, vendors, or third-party integrations, where attackers exploit vulnerabilities in software, hardware, or dependencies to compromise cloud environments or steal sensitive data. Supply chain attacks may involve the compromise of software supply chains, malicious code injections, or the exploitation of trust relationships between cloud service providers and their customers, posing a significant risk to cloud security and data privacy. For example, attackers can infiltrate software supply chains, inject malicious code into legitimate software updates, or compromise third-party libraries used by cloud applications, allowing them to execute arbitrary code, steal data, or gain unauthorized access to cloud environments. In summary, the Cloud Security Threat Landscape presents a diverse array of threats and risks for organizations operating in cloud environments, ranging from data breaches and account hijacking to insider threats, malware, DDoS attacks, and supply chain attacks. By understanding the nature of these threats and adopting a comprehensive approach to cloud security, organizations can mitigate risks, strengthen their security posture, and protect their cloud infrastructure, applications, and data from evolving cyber threats.

Risk Factors in Cloud Adoption are essential considerations for organizations as they transition their IT infrastructure, applications, and services to cloud environments, aiming to leverage the scalability, flexibility, and cost-effectiveness of cloud computing while managing potential risks and challenges. One significant risk factor in cloud adoption is the potential loss of control and visibility over data, applications, and infrastructure when migrating to third-party cloud providers. Organizations may face challenges in maintaining visibility into cloud workloads, data flows, and security controls, leading to concerns about data privacy, compliance, and governance. For example, organizations may use cloud-native monitoring and logging tools such as AWS CloudWatch, Azure Monitor, or Google Cloud Monitoring to gain insights into cloud resource utilization, performance metrics, and security events, enabling them to monitor and manage cloud environments effectively. Another risk factor in cloud adoption is the challenge of data security and protection, where organizations must ensure the confidentiality, integrity, and availability of data stored, processed, or transmitted in cloud environments. Organizations may use encryption technologies such as AWS Key Management Service (KMS), Azure Key Vault, or Google Cloud KMS to encrypt data at rest and in transit, protecting it from unauthorized access and disclosure. Moreover, organizations must address compliance requirements and regulatory obligations when adopting cloud computing, ensuring that their cloud deployments adhere to industry-specific regulations, standards, and best practices. For example, organizations operating in regulated industries such as healthcare, finance, or government must comply with regulations such as the Health Insurance Portability and Accountability Act (HIPAA), the Payment Card Industry Data Security Standard (PCI DSS), or the General Data Protection Regulation (GDPR) when storing, processing, or transmitting sensitive data in the cloud. Additionally, organizations must consider the risk of vendor lock-in when adopting cloud computing, where they become dependent on a single cloud provider for their infrastructure, applications, and services, limiting their ability to migrate workloads or negotiate pricing and terms. To mitigate the risk of vendor lock-in, organizations may adopt a multi-cloud strategy, leveraging multiple cloud providers and services to distribute risk, increase flexibility, and avoid reliance on a single vendor. Moreover, organizations must consider the risk of service outages and disruptions when relying on cloud infrastructure and services for their critical business operations. Cloud providers may experience downtime, performance issues, or service interruptions due to hardware failures, network outages, or cyber attacks, impacting organizations' ability to deliver services to customers and users. To mitigate the risk of service outages, organizations may implement redundant architectures, disaster recovery solutions, and failover mechanisms across multiple cloud regions or availability zones, ensuring high availability and resilience of their cloud deployments. Furthermore, organizations must address the risk of misconfiguration and human error in cloud environments, where misconfigured security settings, access controls, or network configurations may expose sensitive data to unauthorized access or compromise. Organizations may use cloud security posture management (CSPM) tools such as AWS Config, Azure Security Center, or Google Cloud Security Command Center (Cloud SCC) to continuously monitor, assess, and remediate security risks and compliance violations in cloud environments, automating the enforcement of security policies and best practices. Additionally, organizations must consider the risk of insider threats and malicious actors within their own workforce or supply chain, where employees, contractors, or partners may intentionally or unintentionally compromise cloud security through unauthorized access, data theft, or sabotage. To mitigate the risk of insider threats, organizations may implement identity and access management (IAM) controls, least privilege principles, and user behavior analytics (UBA) solutions to detect and respond to suspicious activities and unauthorized access attempts in real-time. In summary, Risk Factors in Cloud Adoption pose significant challenges and considerations for organizations as they embrace cloud computing technologies and migrate their IT infrastructure and services to the cloud. By addressing these risks through proactive risk management strategies, robust security controls, and adherence to best practices and compliance standards, organizations can effectively leverage the benefits of cloud computing while mitigating potential threats and vulnerabilities to their data, applications, and operations.

Risk Identification and Classification are fundamental processes in risk management that involve identifying, analyzing, and categorizing potential risks that may impact an organization's objectives, projects, or operations. One common approach to risk identification is the use of risk assessment methodologies such as SWOT analysis, Delphi technique, or brainstorming sessions, where stakeholders brainstorm potential risks and vulnerabilities related to specific projects, processes, or business activities. For example, organizations may conduct SWOT analysis sessions with project teams or stakeholders to identify internal strengths and weaknesses as well as external opportunities and threats that may affect project success or business continuity. Additionally, organizations may use the Delphi technique, a structured method for gathering and evaluating expert opinions, to identify and prioritize risks based on their likelihood and potential impact. Another approach to risk identification is the use of risk registers or risk matrices, which are structured databases or matrices used to document and categorize identified risks based on their likelihood, impact, and severity. Risk registers typically include information such as the risk description, likelihood, impact, mitigation measures, and responsible parties, enabling organizations to track and manage identified risks throughout the project or operational lifecycle. For example, organizations may use risk registers to document identified risks, assign risk owners, and monitor the status of risk mitigation activities over time. Furthermore, organizations may classify risks based on various criteria such as their nature, origin, or impact on business objectives, enabling them to prioritize and allocate resources effectively to manage high-priority risks. One common classification of risks is based on their nature or source, such as strategic risks, operational risks, financial risks, or compliance risks. Strategic risks relate to uncertainties or threats that may affect an organization's long-term strategic objectives or competitive position in the market. Operational risks pertain to risks associated with the day-to-day operations and processes of an organization, including process failures, human errors, or technology disruptions. Financial risks involve uncertainties or threats that may impact an organization's financial performance, stability, or solvency, such as market volatility, credit risks, or liquidity risks. Compliance risks refer to risks arising from non-compliance with laws, regulations, or industry standards, which may result in legal penalties, reputational damage, or business disruptions. Moreover, organizations may classify risks based on their impact or potential consequences on business objectives, projects, or operations, such as strategic impact, financial impact, operational impact, or reputational impact. Risks with high strategic impact may pose significant threats to an organization's long-term viability, growth, or competitiveness, requiring proactive risk management and mitigation strategies. Risks with high financial impact may affect an organization's financial performance, profitability, or shareholder value, necessitating careful financial planning and risk hedging measures. Risks with high operational impact may disrupt or impair an organization's day-to-day operations, productivity, or service delivery, requiring robust business continuity and disaster recovery plans. Risks with high reputational impact may damage an organization's brand image, customer trust, or stakeholder relationships, necessitating effective crisis management and communication strategies to mitigate reputational harm. Additionally, organizations may classify risks based on their likelihood or probability of occurrence, such as high-risk, medium-risk, or low-risk categories, enabling them to prioritize risk management efforts and resources accordingly. High-risk risks are those with a high likelihood of occurrence and significant potential impact on business objectives, projects, or operations, requiring immediate attention and mitigation actions. Medium-risk risks are those with a moderate likelihood of occurrence and moderate potential impact, requiring proactive monitoring and management to prevent escalation or adverse consequences. Low-risk risks are those with a low likelihood of occurrence and minimal potential impact, which may be accepted or managed with minimal resources or oversight. In summary, Risk Identification and Classification are critical processes in risk management that enable organizations to identify, assess, and prioritize potential risks that may affect their objectives, projects, or operations. By using risk assessment methodologies, risk registers, and risk classification criteria, organizations can systematically identify and categorize risks based on their likelihood, impact, and severity, enabling them to allocate resources effectively and implement targeted risk management strategies to mitigate potential threats and vulnerabilities.

Quantitative and qualitative risk analysis are two complementary approaches used in risk management to assess and evaluate potential risks facing an organization, project, or business activity. Quantitative risk analysis involves the use of numerical or quantitative techniques to measure and quantify risks in terms of probability, impact, and expected monetary losses. One common technique used in quantitative risk analysis is probabilistic risk assessment (PRA), which involves the use of statistical models, simulation tools, or Monte Carlo simulations to assess the likelihood and consequences of identified risks. For example, organizations may use Monte Carlo simulations to model the impact of uncertain variables or inputs on project schedules, budgets, or performance metrics, enabling them to quantify the potential range of outcomes and associated risks. Another technique used in quantitative risk analysis is sensitivity analysis, which involves identifying and analyzing the key variables or factors that have the greatest influence on project outcomes or risk exposure. For example, organizations may conduct sensitivity analyses to assess the impact of changes in market conditions, resource availability, or technology trends on project profitability or success. Additionally, organizations may use scenario analysis, a technique that involves assessing the potential impact of various scenarios or events on project objectives, performance, or outcomes. For example, organizations may develop best-case, worst-case, and most likely scenarios to evaluate the range of potential outcomes and associated risks, enabling them to identify mitigation strategies and contingency plans. Furthermore, organizations may use decision tree analysis, a graphical representation of decision-making processes that incorporates uncertainty and risk, to evaluate the expected value of different decision alternatives and their associated risks. For example, organizations may use decision trees to assess investment decisions, product development strategies, or project planning scenarios, considering the probabilities and consequences of various outcomes. In contrast, qualitative risk analysis involves the use of subjective or qualitative techniques to assess and evaluate risks based on expert judgment, experience, or intuition. One common technique used in qualitative risk analysis is risk scoring or risk ranking, which involves assigning subjective scores or rankings to identified risks based on their likelihood, impact, and severity. For example, organizations may use risk matrices or heat maps to visually represent and prioritize risks based on their likelihood and consequences, enabling them to focus on high-priority risks that require immediate attention or mitigation actions. Another technique used in qualitative risk analysis is risk categorization, which involves grouping identified risks into categories or themes based on their common attributes, characteristics, or sources. For example, organizations may categorize risks into strategic, operational, financial, or compliance categories to facilitate risk assessment and management processes. Additionally, organizations may use risk workshops or brainstorming sessions to engage stakeholders and subject matter experts in identifying, discussing, and evaluating potential risks and opportunities. For example, organizations may convene cross-functional teams or project groups to brainstorm and assess risks associated with specific business initiatives, projects, or activities, enabling them to leverage collective knowledge and expertise to identify and prioritize risks effectively. Furthermore, organizations may use risk registers or risk databases to document and track identified risks, including their descriptions, likelihood, impact, mitigation measures, and responsible parties.

For example, organizations may use risk registers to capture and monitor risks throughout the project or operational lifecycle, enabling them to proactively manage and mitigate risks as they arise. In summary, Quantitative and qualitative risk analysis are essential components of effective risk management, enabling organizations to assess, evaluate, and prioritize potential risks based on their likelihood, impact, and severity. By using a combination of quantitative and qualitative techniques, organizations can gain valuable insights into their risk exposure and develop targeted risk management strategies to mitigate threats, capitalize on opportunities, and enhance business resilience and performance.

Risk treatment options are crucial strategies employed by organizations to manage and mitigate identified risks effectively, ensuring the protection of assets, the achievement of objectives, and the optimization of opportunities. One primary risk treatment option is risk avoidance, which involves eliminating or avoiding activities, processes, or situations that could potentially expose the organization to risks. For instance, if an organization identifies a high-risk project that could significantly impact its financial stability or reputation, it may choose to avoid proceeding with the project altogether, thus eliminating the associated risks. Another risk treatment option is risk reduction, which aims to decrease the likelihood or impact of identified risks through proactive measures and controls. An example of risk reduction is implementing security controls and protocols to mitigate cybersecurity threats, such as installing firewalls, antivirus software, and intrusion detection systems to protect against malicious attacks. Additionally, organizations may implement redundancy and backup systems to minimize the impact of potential disruptions or failures, ensuring business continuity and resilience. Furthermore, risk transfer is a common risk treatment option where organizations transfer the financial consequences of risks to third parties, such as insurance companies or subcontractors. For example, organizations may purchase insurance policies to cover losses resulting from natural disasters, accidents, or legal liabilities, transferring the financial burden of such risks to the insurance provider. Moreover, risk acceptance is a risk treatment option where organizations acknowledge and accept certain risks as unavoidable or acceptable within predefined tolerance levels. This approach is often adopted for risks with low likelihood or impact, where the cost of mitigation outweighs the potential benefits. For example, organizations may accept the risk of minor IT system outages during non-critical periods, prioritizing resources for more significant risks or strategic initiatives. Additionally, risk-sharing is a collaborative risk treatment option where organizations partner with other entities to collectively address and mitigate shared risks. For instance, organizations may form consortiums or alliances to pool resources, expertise, and capabilities to tackle common risks, such as cybersecurity threats or supply chain disruptions. Furthermore, contingency planning is a proactive risk treatment option where organizations develop and implement predefined response plans and procedures to address potential risks and emergencies. For example, organizations may create business continuity plans (BCPs) and disaster recovery plans (DRPs) to mitigate the impact of natural disasters, cyber-attacks, or other disruptive events, ensuring timely response and recovery efforts.

Additionally, organizations may conduct scenario-based exercises and simulations to test the effectiveness of contingency plans and identify areas for improvement. Moreover, risk monitoring and review are essential risk treatment options that involve ongoing surveillance and evaluation of identified risks, ensuring that risk management strategies remain effective and responsive to changing circumstances. Organizations may establish key performance indicators (KPIs), thresholds, and triggers to monitor risk exposure and performance, enabling timely intervention and adjustments as needed. Furthermore, regular risk assessments, audits, and reviews are conducted to evaluate the effectiveness of risk treatment measures and identify emerging risks or gaps in controls. In summary, Risk treatment options are essential components of effective risk management, enabling organizations to proactively identify, assess, and address potential risks to achieve their objectives and enhance business resilience. By employing a combination of risk avoidance, risk reduction, risk transfer, risk acceptance, risk-sharing, contingency planning, and risk monitoring strategies, organizations can mitigate threats, capitalize on opportunities, and optimize their risk posture in a dynamic and uncertain business environment.

Risk transfer and acceptance are essential components of risk management strategies employed by organizations to mitigate potential threats and vulnerabilities effectively, ensuring the continuity of operations and the achievement of business objectives. One primary method of risk transfer is through insurance policies, where organizations transfer the financial consequences of specific risks to insurance providers in exchange for premium payments. For instance, organizations may purchase property insurance to protect against damages from natural disasters such as floods, earthquakes, or hurricanes, transferring the financial burden of such events to the insurance company. Similarly, liability insurance can safeguard organizations against legal claims and lawsuits resulting from accidents, injuries, or negligence, providing financial protection and peace of mind. Additionally, organizations may utilize contractual agreements and indemnification clauses to transfer risks to third parties, such as vendors, suppliers, or subcontractors. For example, organizations may include indemnity provisions in contracts with service providers to hold them responsible for any losses or damages caused by their actions or omissions, thereby transferring the associated risks to the contracted party. Moreover, organizations may engage in risk-sharing arrangements and partnerships to distribute and mitigate risks collectively. For instance, joint ventures, consortiums, or alliances allow organizations to pool resources, expertise, and capabilities to address common risks and challenges more effectively. By sharing risks with other entities, organizations can reduce their individual exposure and enhance their resilience in a dynamic and uncertain environment. Furthermore, risk acceptance is a strategic decision made by organizations to acknowledge and tolerate certain risks within predefined tolerance levels. This approach is typically adopted for risks with low likelihood or impact, where the cost of mitigation exceeds the potential benefits. For example, organizations may accept the risk of minor IT system disruptions during non-critical periods, prioritizing resources for more significant risks or strategic initiatives. Additionally, risk acceptance may be necessary when risks are inherent to the nature of the business or industry and cannot be feasibly eliminated or transferred. For instance, organizations operating in highly regulated sectors such as finance, healthcare, or aerospace may face inherent risks related to compliance, security, or safety standards, which must be accepted and managed accordingly. Moreover, risk acceptance requires organizations to establish clear risk appetite and tolerance levels, ensuring that decision-makers understand and agree upon the acceptable level of risk exposure for various activities, projects, or initiatives. By defining risk thresholds and criteria, organizations can effectively prioritize resources, allocate budgets, and implement risk management measures consistent with their strategic objectives and risk tolerance. Additionally, risk acceptance should be accompanied by robust monitoring and oversight mechanisms to track and evaluate risk exposure over time. Regular risk assessments, audits, and reviews are essential to ensure that accepted risks remain within acceptable limits and do not exceed predefined thresholds. Furthermore, organizations should periodically reassess their risk landscape and adjust their risk acceptance strategies accordingly in response to changes in internal or external factors. In summary, Risk transfer and acceptance are critical elements of risk management, enabling organizations to allocate resources effectively, protect against potential losses, and maintain resilience in the face of uncertainty. By leveraging insurance, contractual agreements, partnerships, and informed decision-making processes, organizations can optimize their risk posture and pursue their objectives with confidence in a dynamic and competitive business environment.

Vendor risk assessment frameworks are systematic methodologies employed by organizations to evaluate and manage the risks associated with their vendors, suppliers, and third-party service providers, ensuring the integrity, security, and reliability of outsourced products and services. One commonly used vendor risk assessment framework is the Shared Assessments Program, which provides standardized assessment tools and best practices for evaluating vendor controls and compliance with industry standards and regulations. The Shared Assessments Program offers a range of assessment tools, including the Standardized Information Gathering (SIG) questionnaire, which enables organizations to collect detailed information about vendor security controls, policies, and practices. Additionally, the Shared Assessments Program provides the Standardized Control Assessment (SCA) tool, which allows organizations to assess the effectiveness of vendor controls against predefined criteria and benchmarks. Another widely adopted vendor risk assessment framework is the National Institute of Standards and Technology (NIST) Cybersecurity Framework, which provides a flexible and risk-based approach to managing cybersecurity risks across organizations and their supply chains. The NIST Cybersecurity Framework consists of five core functions: Identify, Protect, Detect, Respond, and Recover, which organizations can use to assess and improve their cybersecurity posture and vendor management practices. Furthermore, the International Organization for Standardization (ISO) 27001 standard provides a comprehensive framework for implementing and managing information security management systems (ISMS), including vendor risk management processes. ISO 27001 emphasizes the importance of assessing vendor risks as part of the organization's overall risk management strategy and requires organizations to establish controls and procedures for evaluating and monitoring vendor performance and compliance. Additionally, organizations may develop their proprietary vendor risk assessment frameworks tailored to their specific industry, regulatory requirements, and risk appetite. These custom frameworks typically include a combination of risk identification, assessment, mitigation, and monitoring processes designed to address the unique challenges and vulnerabilities associated with vendor relationships. Moreover, vendor risk assessment frameworks typically involve several key steps, including vendor identification and categorization, risk profiling and prioritization, assessment planning and execution, control evaluation, and ongoing monitoring and review. Organizations start by identifying and categorizing their vendors based on factors such as criticality, access to sensitive data or systems, and potential impact on business operations. Once vendors are classified, organizations conduct risk profiling and prioritization exercises to assess the inherent risks associated with each vendor and prioritize them for further assessment and mitigation efforts. Subsequently, organizations develop assessment plans detailing the scope, objectives, methodologies, and timelines for evaluating vendor controls and compliance with predefined criteria, standards, and regulations. This may involve sending out questionnaires, conducting onsite audits or assessments, reviewing documentation and evidence provided by vendors, and engaging in discussions or interviews to gather additional information. Additionally, organizations use various tools and techniques to evaluate vendor controls and practices, such as penetration testing, vulnerability scanning, security assessments, and compliance reviews. CLI commands such as "nmap" or "nikto" can be used for network scanning and vulnerability assessment, while tools like "OpenVAS" or "Qualys" can automate the vulnerability management process and provide detailed reports on security weaknesses and exposures. Moreover, organizations may utilize third-party risk intelligence services and databases to gather information about vendor reputations, security incidents, regulatory violations, and other relevant risk factors. Once assessments are complete, organizations analyze the findings, identify gaps and deficiencies, and work with vendors to develop remediation plans and corrective actions to address identified issues. Additionally, organizations establish monitoring and review processes to track vendor performance, compliance, and security posture over time, ensuring that risks are effectively managed and mitigated throughout the vendor lifecycle. In summary, Vendor risk assessment frameworks are essential tools for organizations to evaluate and manage the risks associated with their vendors and third-party service providers effectively. By leveraging standardized frameworks, industry best practices, and risk management methodologies, organizations can enhance transparency, accountability, and trust in their vendor relationships, safeguarding against potential threats and vulnerabilities and maintaining the integrity and resilience of their operations and supply chains.

Third-party risk monitoring techniques play a pivotal role in contemporary risk management strategies, enabling organizations to effectively assess, track, and mitigate risks associated with their vendors, suppliers, and service providers. One widely utilized technique is continuous monitoring, which involves the real-time or near-real-time assessment of third-party activities, performance, and security posture to identify potential risks and anomalies promptly. Continuous monitoring leverages various tools and technologies to collect and analyze data from multiple sources, including network traffic, logs, security alerts, and external threat intelligence feeds. These tools can include Security Information and Event Management (SIEM) systems, Intrusion Detection Systems (IDS), Endpoint Detection and Response (EDR) solutions, and threat intelligence platforms, which aggregate and correlate data to detect suspicious behavior or indicators of compromise. Additionally, organizations can employ automated scanning and assessment tools to periodically evaluate third-party systems, networks, and applications for vulnerabilities, misconfigurations, and compliance gaps. Vulnerability scanners such as Nessus, OpenVAS, or Qualys can be deployed to identify known vulnerabilities in third-party assets, while configuration management tools like Ansible or Puppet can automate the enforcement of security controls and best practices across distributed environments. Furthermore, organizations can implement risk scoring and rating mechanisms to prioritize and classify third-party risks based on their potential impact, likelihood, and criticality to business operations. Risk scoring models may incorporate factors such as the sensitivity of data or systems involved, the nature of the services provided, the geographic location of vendors, and historical performance or incident data. By assigning numerical scores or ratings to different risk factors, organizations can effectively prioritize their risk mitigation efforts and allocate resources accordingly. Moreover, organizations can leverage external risk intelligence services and databases to augment their internal monitoring efforts and gain insights into third-party risks across various dimensions. These services provide comprehensive assessments of vendors' security postures, compliance with industry standards and regulations, financial stability, and reputation in the marketplace. By leveraging external intelligence, organizations can supplement their internal assessments with independent, unbiased evaluations of third-party risks, enhancing their overall risk visibility and decision-making capabilities. Additionally, organizations can establish contractual agreements and service level agreements (SLAs) with third-party vendors to define expectations, responsibilities, and performance metrics related to risk management and security. These agreements may include provisions for regular reporting, audits, and reviews to ensure compliance with contractual obligations and regulatory requirements. Moreover, organizations can conduct periodic audits and assessments of third-party vendors to validate their adherence to contractual terms, industry standards, and regulatory mandates. These audits may involve onsite visits, interviews, documentation reviews, and technical assessments to evaluate the effectiveness of vendor controls and practices. Additionally, organizations can implement incident response and communication protocols to facilitate timely and coordinated responses to security incidents or breaches involving third-party vendors. These protocols should outline the roles, responsibilities, and escalation procedures for all parties involved, ensuring a swift and effective response to mitigate potential damages and restore normal operations. Furthermore, organizations can establish governance structures and oversight mechanisms to monitor and manage third-party risks at the executive and board levels. This may involve the creation of dedicated committees or working groups tasked with overseeing vendor relationships, conducting risk assessments, and making informed decisions about risk acceptance, mitigation, or termination. By integrating third-party risk management into broader governance frameworks, organizations can ensure accountability, transparency, and alignment with strategic objectives and risk appetite. In summary, Third-party risk monitoring techniques are essential components of modern risk management practices, enabling organizations to proactively identify, assess, and mitigate risks associated with their extended enterprise ecosystem. By leveraging continuous monitoring, automated scanning, risk scoring, external intelligence, contractual agreements, audits, incident response protocols, and governance structures, organizations can effectively manage third-party risks and safeguard their operations, reputation, and assets from potential threats and vulnerabilities.

Key legal terms in cloud contracts are crucial elements that define the rights, responsibilities, and obligations of parties involved in cloud computing agreements, governing the use, access, and management of cloud services and resources. One essential legal term is the Service Level Agreement (SLA), which outlines the agreed-upon levels of service availability, performance, and support provided by the cloud service provider (CSP). SLAs typically include metrics such as uptime guarantees, response times, and service credits or penalties for failure to meet specified performance targets. Another critical term is the Acceptable Use Policy (AUP), which defines the acceptable and prohibited uses of cloud services and resources, outlining restrictions on activities such as hacking, spamming, copyright infringement, and other forms of abuse or misuse. AUPs help prevent unauthorized or malicious behavior and ensure compliance with legal and regulatory requirements. Moreover, cloud contracts often include provisions related to data ownership and intellectual property rights, clarifying which party retains ownership of data uploaded, processed, or stored in the cloud environment and delineating rights and licenses for using customer data, software, or proprietary information. These provisions help protect the interests of both parties and mitigate risks related to data security, privacy, and intellectual property infringement. Additionally, cloud contracts may contain indemnification clauses, which allocate liability and responsibility for damages, losses, or legal claims arising from breaches of contract, negligence, or other wrongful acts. Indemnification clauses typically specify the scope of indemnity, limitations of liability, and procedures for notifying and resolving disputes between the parties. Furthermore, confidentiality and data protection clauses are essential legal terms in cloud contracts, establishing obligations for safeguarding sensitive information and personal data shared or processed in the cloud environment. These clauses may include requirements for encryption, access controls, data breach notification, and compliance with privacy laws and regulations, such as the General Data Protection Regulation (GDPR) in the European Union or the Health Insurance Portability and Accountability Act (HIPAA) in the United States. Additionally, cloud contracts often incorporate termination and exit management provisions, outlining the conditions under which either party may terminate the agreement and the process for transitioning data, services, and resources upon termination or expiration of the contract. These provisions help ensure a smooth and orderly transition of operations and mitigate risks associated with service disruptions or vendor lock-in. Moreover, liability and warranty disclaimers are common legal terms in cloud contracts, limiting the liability of CSPs for damages, losses, or disruptions caused by factors beyond their control, such as force majeure events, network outages, or security breaches. These disclaimers clarify the extent of the CSP's responsibility and help manage expectations regarding service availability, reliability, and performance. Additionally, jurisdiction and governing law clauses specify the legal framework and venue for resolving disputes or enforcing contractual rights and obligations, establishing which jurisdiction's laws apply and where legal proceedings must be initiated. These clauses help ensure legal certainty, predictability, and consistency in contract interpretation and enforcement across different jurisdictions. Furthermore, audit and compliance requirements are essential legal terms in cloud contracts, enabling customers to verify CSPs' adherence to contractual terms, industry standards, and regulatory requirements through periodic audits, assessments, or certifications. These requirements help maintain transparency, accountability, and trust in cloud service relationships and ensure compliance with legal, regulatory, and industry-specific requirements. In summary, Key legal terms in cloud contracts play a crucial role in defining the rights, responsibilities, and obligations of parties involved in cloud computing agreements, ensuring clarity, transparency, and enforceability of contractual terms and mitigating risks associated with data security, privacy, compliance, and liability. SLA management and enforcement are critical aspects of cloud service delivery and governance, ensuring that service providers meet their contractual commitments regarding performance, availability, and support. One fundamental aspect of SLA management is defining clear and measurable service level objectives (SLOs) that align with the organization's business requirements and expectations. This involves identifying key performance indicators (KPIs) and establishing target thresholds for metrics such as uptime, response times, and service availability, which serve as the basis for SLA agreements. Once SLOs are established, organizations must monitor and track service performance against these objectives using monitoring and management tools such as Prometheus, Grafana, or Nagios. These tools collect data on various aspects of service delivery, including server uptime, network latency, and application response times, allowing organizations to assess compliance with SLA requirements and identify performance issues or deviations from agreed-upon targets. In addition to monitoring service performance, organizations must establish processes and procedures for reporting and documenting SLA breaches or incidents. This may involve setting up incident management systems or ticketing platforms such as Jira or ServiceNow to track and prioritize SLA-related issues, escalate critical incidents, and coordinate responses across different teams or departments. Moreover, organizations may implement automated alerting and notification mechanisms to proactively alert stakeholders about potential SLA breaches or performance degradation, enabling timely intervention and remediation actions. These alerts can be configured using tools like Prometheus Alertmanager or Nagios Event Handlers, which trigger notifications via email, SMS, or other communication channels when predefined thresholds are exceeded. Furthermore, SLA management involves regular review and analysis of service performance data to identify trends, patterns, and areas for improvement. This may include conducting root cause analysis (RCA) to investigate the underlying causes of SLA breaches or recurring incidents, identifying systemic issues, and implementing corrective actions or preventive measures to address them. Additionally, organizations must ensure that SLA agreements are enforceable and legally binding, with clear mechanisms for recourse in the event of non-compliance or disputes. This may involve including penalty clauses, service credits, or liquidated damages provisions in SLA contracts to incentivize service providers to meet their obligations and compensate customers for any breaches or failures to deliver on promised service levels. Moreover, organizations can leverage Service Level Management (SLM) platforms or SLA management software solutions to automate SLA tracking, enforcement, and reporting processes. These platforms centralize SLA management activities, streamline communication between stakeholders, and provide real-time visibility into service performance and compliance status. Popular SLM tools include ServiceNow IT Service Management (ITSM), Freshservice, and SolarWinds Service Desk. Furthermore, organizations may implement governance frameworks and oversight mechanisms to ensure accountability and transparency in SLA management and enforcement. This may involve establishing SLA review boards or governance committees responsible for reviewing SLA performance, resolving disputes, and driving continuous improvement initiatives to enhance service quality and customer satisfaction. Additionally, organizations can conduct regular audits and assessments of SLA compliance and effectiveness to identify gaps, bottlenecks, or areas *for optimization. These audits may involve internal or external stakeholders, including customers, auditors, or regulatory bodies, who evaluate SLA adherence against predefined criteria, benchmarks, or industry standards. In summary, SLA management and enforcement are essential components of effective cloud service delivery and governance, ensuring that service providers meet their contractual commitments and deliver consistent, reliable, and high-quality services to customers. By defining clear SLOs, monitoring service performance, establishing incident management processes, enforcing SLA agreements, leveraging automation tools, and implementing governance frameworks, organizations can proactively manage SLAs, mitigate risks, and drive continuous improvement in service delivery and customer satisfaction.*

Compliance requirements in cloud environments are multifaceted and demand meticulous attention to ensure adherence to various regulations, standards, and industry best practices governing data protection, privacy, security, and other aspects of cloud operations. One fundamental compliance consideration in cloud environments is data privacy, particularly concerning the collection, storage, processing, and transmission of personally identifiable information (PII) or sensitive data. Compliance with data privacy regulations such as the General Data Protection Regulation (GDPR) in the European Union, the California Consumer Privacy Act (CCPA) in the United States, or the Personal Data Protection Act (PDPA) in Singapore is paramount for organizations handling personal data in the cloud. To achieve compliance with these regulations, organizations must implement appropriate data protection measures, such as encryption, access controls, pseudonymization, and data residency restrictions, to safeguard personal data and ensure privacy rights are respected. Another critical compliance area in cloud environments is data security, encompassing a range of controls and practices designed to protect data from unauthorized access, disclosure, alteration, or destruction. Compliance with data security standards such as the ISO/IEC 27001, NIST SP 800-53, or the Payment Card Industry Data Security Standard (PCI DSS) requires organizations to implement robust security controls, including network segmentation, encryption, intrusion detection, and vulnerability management, to mitigate security risks and safeguard sensitive information in the cloud. Moreover, regulatory compliance in cloud environments extends beyond data privacy and security to include industry-specific regulations and standards governing sectors such as healthcare, finance, government, and telecommunications. For example, organizations in the healthcare industry must comply with the Health Insurance Portability and Accountability Act (HIPAA) in the United States or the Health Information Privacy (HIP) Code in Australia, which impose stringent requirements for protecting patient health information (PHI) and ensuring the confidentiality, integrity, and availability of healthcare data stored or processed in the cloud. Similarly, financial institutions must adhere to regulations such as the Sarbanes-Oxley Act (SOX), the Payment Services Directive (PSD2), or the Basel III Accord, which mandate strict controls and reporting requirements to safeguard financial data, prevent fraud, and maintain market stability. Additionally, government agencies and contractors operating in the cloud must comply with regulatory frameworks such as the Federal Risk and Authorization Management Program (FedRAMP) in the United States, the Cybersecurity Maturity Model

Certification (CMMC), or the European Union Agency for Cybersecurity (ENISA) guidelines, which provide guidance on securing cloud services and managing cyber risks in public sector environments. Furthermore, international data transfer and localization requirements present compliance challenges for organizations operating in multiple jurisdictions or regions with divergent data protection laws and regulations. Cross-border data transfers must comply with legal mechanisms such as the EU-US Privacy Shield, Standard Contractual Clauses (SCCs), Binding Corporate Rules (BCRs), or data localization requirements imposed by certain countries, which dictate where data can be stored, processed, or transferred based on jurisdictional boundaries or sovereignty concerns. Moreover, cloud service providers play a crucial role in assisting organizations with compliance efforts by offering compliant infrastructure, services, and assurances through certifications, attestations, and audit reports. Providers such as Amazon Web Services (AWS), Microsoft Azure, and Google Cloud Platform (GCP) offer compliance programs and services that align with various regulatory requirements and industry standards, enabling customers to build and operate compliant cloud environments effectively. Additionally, organizations must establish governance frameworks, policies, and procedures to ensure ongoing compliance with evolving regulatory requirements and industry best practices. This may involve appointing compliance officers or teams responsible for monitoring regulatory changes, conducting risk assessments, implementing controls, and coordinating audit activities to demonstrate compliance and address any non-compliance issues promptly. Furthermore, organizations can leverage cloud-native compliance management tools and services to automate compliance monitoring, reporting, and remediation processes, streamlining compliance efforts and reducing manual overhead. These tools, such as AWS Config, Azure Policy, or Google Cloud Security Command Center (SCC), provide continuous visibility into compliance status, identify configuration drift, enforce policy compliance, and generate audit reports to demonstrate adherence to regulatory requirements. In summary, compliance requirements in cloud environments are diverse and complex, encompassing data privacy, security, industry-specific regulations, international data transfers, and provider assurance considerations. By implementing robust controls, leveraging cloud provider services, staying abreast of regulatory changes, and adopting automated compliance management tools, organizations can effectively navigate compliance challenges and build secure, compliant, and resilient cloud environments tailored to their business needs.

Regulatory compliance frameworks play a pivotal role in guiding organizations across various industries *towards adherence to legal requirements, industry standards, and best practices to ensure the security, integrity, and confidentiality of data and operations. One of the most widely recognized compliance frameworks is the Payment Card Industry Data Security Standard (PCI DSS), which governs the handling of cardholder data and mandates specific security controls for organizations that process, store, or transmit payment card information. To achieve PCI DSS compliance, organizations must implement measures such as network segmentation, encryption, access controls, and regular security testing to protect cardholder data and maintain a secure payment environment. Additionally, compliance with the Health Insurance Portability and Accountability Act (HIPAA) is imperative for healthcare organizations to safeguard protected health information (PHI) and ensure patient privacy and confidentiality. HIPAA sets forth stringent requirements for the security and privacy of PHI, including access controls, audit trails, risk assessments, and breach notification procedures, to prevent unauthorized access, disclosure, or misuse of sensitive health data. Moreover, the General Data Protection Regulation (GDPR) imposes strict obligations on organizations handling personal data of European Union (EU) residents, regardless of their location, to protect individuals' privacy rights and ensure transparent and lawful processing of personal data. GDPR compliance entails measures such as data encryption, pseudonymization, data protection impact assessments (DPIAs), and the appointment of a Data Protection Officer (DPO) to oversee compliance efforts and facilitate communication with data protection authorities. Furthermore, the Sarbanes-Oxley Act (SOX) establishes requirements for financial reporting and corporate governance to enhance transparency, accountability, and integrity in financial disclosures and prevent accounting fraud or misconduct. SOX compliance involves controls such as segregation of duties, financial reporting controls, internal audits, and whistleblower protection mechanisms to ensure the accuracy and reliability of financial information and protect shareholders' interests. Additionally, the Federal Information Security Management Act (FISMA) mandates federal agencies to develop, implement, and maintain information security programs to protect sensitive government information and systems from cyber threats and vulnerabilities. FISMA compliance involves conducting risk assessments, developing security plans, implementing security controls, and undergoing regular security assessments and audits to ensure the effectiveness of information security programs and safeguard federal assets. Furthermore, industry-specific compliance frameworks such as the Federal Risk and Authorization Management Program (FedRAMP) are essential for cloud service providers (CSPs) seeking to offer cloud services to federal agencies. FedRAMP establishes security requirements and provides a standardized approach for assessing, authorizing, and monitoring cloud services' security posture to ensure they meet federal security standards and support government missions. Moreover, international compliance frameworks such as the ISO/IEC 27001 series provide a globally recognized framework for establishing, implementing, maintaining, and continually improving an information security management system (ISMS) to manage risks and protect information assets. ISO/IEC 27001 compliance involves conducting risk assessments, implementing security controls, conducting internal audits, and undergoing external audits to achieve certification and demonstrate compliance with international security standards. Additionally, industry-specific compliance frameworks such as the Payment Services Directive (PSD2) for the banking and financial services sector and the North American Electric Reliability Corporation Critical Infrastructure Protection (NERC CIP) standards for the energy sector impose specific requirements to protect sensitive financial data and critical infrastructure assets from cyber threats and ensure the reliability and security of essential services. Furthermore, emerging compliance frameworks such as the California Consumer Privacy Act (CCPA) and the Singapore Personal Data Protection Act (PDPA) reflect the growing emphasis on data privacy and protection globally and compel organizations to enhance their data governance practices, transparency, and accountability in handling personal data. In summary, regulatory compliance frameworks serve as essential guidelines for organizations to ensure they meet legal, regulatory, and industry requirements, mitigate risks, and protect sensitive information and critical assets from cyber threats and vulnerabilities. By adopting a proactive approach to compliance, implementing robust controls and security measures, and leveraging best practices and standards, organizations can demonstrate their commitment to regulatory compliance, build trust with stakeholders, and safeguard their reputation and brand integrity in an increasingly interconnected and regulated business environment.*

Cloud disaster recovery strategies are essential components of modern business continuity plans, enabling organizations to mitigate the impact of unforeseen events such as natural disasters, cyberattacks, hardware failures, or human errors on their IT infrastructure and operations. These strategies involve implementing proactive measures to ensure the rapid recovery of critical systems, data, and applications in the event of a disaster, minimizing downtime, data loss, and financial losses. One widely adopted cloud disaster recovery strategy is the use of backup and replication solutions to create redundant copies of data and applications in geographically dispersed locations, ensuring resilience and availability in case of a disaster. Organizations can leverage cloud-based backup services such as Amazon S3, Azure Blob Storage, or Google Cloud Storage to store backups securely and cost-effectively, leveraging features like versioning, encryption, and lifecycle management to meet their specific recovery objectives. CLI commands, such as aws s3 cp or az storage blob upload, can be used to upload data to cloud storage repositories, while automation tools like AWS Lambda or Azure Functions can automate backup tasks and enforce backup policies based on predefined schedules or triggers. Additionally, organizations can implement disaster recovery as a service (DRaaS) solutions offered by cloud providers or third-party vendors, which provide fully managed, scalable, and resilient disaster recovery capabilities without the need for upfront investment in hardware or infrastructure. DRaaS solutions replicate entire virtual machines or application workloads to the cloud, enabling rapid failover and failback in the event of a disaster, with minimal disruption to business operations. Using CLI commands like az vm create or gcloud compute instances create, organizations can provision virtual machines or resources in the cloud to replicate their on-premises environments, while DRaaS platforms automate replication, monitoring, and recovery processes to ensure seamless failover and data integrity. Furthermore, organizations can implement multi-cloud disaster recovery strategies to leverage redundancy and diversity across multiple cloud providers, mitigating the risk of vendor lock-in, service outages, or regional disasters that may impact a single cloud provider. By replicating data and workloads across different cloud environments, organizations can enhance resilience, availability, and disaster recovery readiness, leveraging CLI commands like aws ec2 create-image or gcloud compute images create to create machine images or snapshots for cross-cloud replication and failover. Moreover, organizations should regularly test their cloud disaster recovery plans through tabletop exercises, simulations, or live drills to validate the effectiveness of their strategies, identify gaps or weaknesses, and refine their response procedures accordingly. Testing can involve orchestrating failover scenarios, simulating data loss or corruption, and evaluating the recovery time objectives (RTOs) and recovery point objectives (RPOs) to ensure they align with business requirements and regulatory compliance mandates. CLI commands like aws ec2 run-instances or az vm start can be used to initiate failover tests and validate the integrity and availability of replicated resources in the cloud environment. Additionally, organizations should consider implementing continuous monitoring and automated alerting mechanisms to detect potential issues or anomalies that may affect the integrity or availability of their disaster recovery infrastructure, allowing them to respond promptly and proactively to mitigate risks and prevent disruptions. By adopting robust cloud disaster recovery strategies and leveraging CLI commands, automation, and testing methodologies, organizations can enhance their resilience, minimize downtime, and safeguard their critical business operations and data against the impact of disasters or disruptions in the cloud environment.

Cloud-based business continuity solutions have become increasingly vital for organizations seeking to ensure uninterrupted operations and mitigate the impact of disruptions or disasters on their business processes, applications, and data. These solutions leverage cloud computing technologies and services to provide resilient, scalable, and cost-effective continuity strategies that enable organizations to maintain critical functions and services during adverse events. One key component of cloud-based business continuity solutions is the use of cloud storage and backup services to create redundant copies of data and applications, ensuring data integrity, availability, and recoverability in the event of a disaster or outage. Organizations can leverage cloud storage platforms such as Amazon S3, Azure Blob Storage, or Google Cloud Storage to store backups securely and efficiently, leveraging features like versioning, encryption, and geo-replication to protect against data loss and corruption. The process of backing up data to the cloud can be automated using scripting or orchestration tools, with CLI commands like aws s3 cp or az storage blob upload allowing organizations to upload data to cloud storage repositories programmatically. Additionally, cloud-based backup solutions often offer advanced features such as deduplication, compression, and incremental backups to optimize storage utilization and reduce backup windows, enabling organizations to meet stringent recovery point objectives (RPOs) and recovery time objectives (RTOs). Another critical aspect of cloud-based business continuity solutions is the implementation of disaster recovery as a service (DRaaS) platforms, which provide fully managed, scalable, and resilient disaster recovery capabilities in the cloud. DRaaS solutions replicate entire virtual machines or application workloads to the cloud, enabling organizations to failover rapidly in the event of a disaster or outage, with minimal disruption to business operations. CLI commands such as aws ec2 create-image or az vm capture can be used to create machine images or snapshots for replication to the cloud, while automation tools like AWS Lambda or Azure Functions can orchestrate failover processes and enforce recovery policies based on predefined triggers or conditions. Additionally, DRaaS platforms often include features such as automated failover testing, recovery plan orchestration, and continuous monitoring to ensure the integrity and availability of replicated resources and data. Moreover, cloud-based business continuity solutions offer organizations the flexibility to implement hybrid or multi-cloud architectures, leveraging redundancy and diversity across multiple cloud providers to enhance resilience and mitigate the risk of vendor lock-in, service outages, or regional disasters. By replicating data and workloads across different cloud environments, organizations can ensure business continuity and data protection while optimizing costs, performance, and compliance. CLI commands like gcloud compute instances create or az vm start can be used to provision resources in different cloud environments for cross-cloud replication and failover, with automation frameworks like Terraform or Ansible facilitating the deployment and management of multi-cloud architectures. Additionally, organizations should regularly test and validate their cloud-based business continuity plans through tabletop exercises, simulations, or live drills to identify gaps, assess the effectiveness of recovery procedures, and refine their strategies accordingly. Testing can involve orchestrating failover scenarios, simulating data loss or corruption, and evaluating the RPOs and RTOs to ensure they align with business requirements and regulatory mandates. Continuous monitoring and automated alerting mechanisms should also be implemented to detect and respond to potential issues or anomalies that may affect the integrity or availability of critical systems and data. In summary, cloud-based business continuity solutions offer organizations robust, scalable, and cost-effective strategies to ensure uninterrupted operations and mitigate the impact of disruptions or disasters on their business continuity. By leveraging cloud storage, backup, DRaaS, and multi-cloud architectures, organizations can enhance resilience, minimize downtime, and safeguard critical data and applications against a wide range of threats and vulnerabilities in the dynamic and evolving landscape of cloud computing.

Cloud incident response frameworks are essential for organizations operating in cloud environments to effectively detect, respond to, and recover from security incidents and breaches. These frameworks provide structured methodologies, procedures, and guidelines for orchestrating incident response activities, enabling organizations to minimize the impact of security incidents on their operations, reputation, and customer trust. One widely adopted incident response framework is the NIST Computer Security Incident Handling Guide, which offers a comprehensive and systematic approach to incident detection, analysis, containment, eradication, and recovery. Organizations can leverage the NIST framework to establish incident response teams, define roles and responsibilities, and develop incident response plans tailored to their specific cloud environment and business requirements. The incident response process typically begins with the identification of security incidents through proactive monitoring, logging, and alerting mechanisms deployed across cloud infrastructure and services. Tools like Amazon CloudWatch, Azure Monitor, or Google Cloud Security Command Center can be configured to collect and analyze logs, metrics, and events generated by cloud resources, applications, and network traffic, allowing organizations to detect anomalies, unauthorized access attempts, or suspicious activities indicative of a security incident. Once an incident is detected, organizations must initiate the response phase by activating the incident response team and executing predefined response procedures outlined in the incident response plan. This may involve isolating affected systems or resources, collecting evidence for forensic analysis, and containing the spread of the incident to prevent further damage or compromise. CLI commands such as aws ec2 isolate-instance or az network nsg rule create can be used to implement network segmentation or access controls to isolate compromised assets or limit lateral movement within the cloud environment. Furthermore, incident response teams should prioritize the containment and eradication of the incident by remediating vulnerabilities, applying patches, or deploying compensating controls to mitigate ongoing threats and vulnerabilities. Automated response actions can be triggered using cloud-native security tools or third-party orchestration platforms to streamline incident containment and reduce manual intervention. For example, AWS Lambda functions or Azure Logic Apps can be configured to automate the execution of remediation scripts or playbooks in response to specific security events or triggers detected in the cloud environment. Additionally, organizations should leverage threat intelligence feeds, security information and event management (SIEM) solutions, and incident response playbooks to enrich incident data, correlate security events, and prioritize response efforts based on the severity and impact of the incident. Collaboration and communication are key components of effective incident response, with incident response teams often relying on dedicated communication channels, incident collaboration platforms, or incident response management tools to coordinate response activities, share critical information, and facilitate decision-making processes. CLI commands such as aws sns publish or az monitor alert create can be used to send real-time notifications or alerts to incident response team members, stakeholders, or management personnel, keeping them informed about the status of the incident and any response actions taken. Moreover, organizations should conduct post-incident reviews and analysis to identify lessons learned, root causes, and areas for improvement in their incident response processes and procedures. This may involve conducting post-mortem meetings, analyzing incident data and metrics, and documenting findings and recommendations for future incident response planning and training. By continuously refining and maturing their incident response capabilities, organizations can enhance their resilience to security threats and breaches in the dynamic and evolving landscape of cloud computing. Incident response playbooks for cloud environments are essential documents that outline predefined steps, procedures, and actions to be taken in response to security incidents and breaches occurring within cloud infrastructure and services. These playbooks serve as a roadmap for incident response teams, providing guidance on how to effectively detect, analyze, contain, eradicate, and recover from security incidents in the cloud. Developing comprehensive incident response playbooks tailored to the unique characteristics and challenges of cloud environments is crucial for organizations to minimize the impact of security incidents, mitigate risks, and maintain business continuity. The creation of incident response playbooks typically begins with a thorough assessment of the organization's cloud architecture, resources, applications, and data assets to identify potential security risks, threats, and vulnerabilities that could lead to security incidents. Incident response teams collaborate with cloud architects, security engineers, and other stakeholders to understand the organization's cloud environment, including its infrastructure-as-a-service (IaaS), platform-as-a-service (PaaS), and software-as-a-service (SaaS) deployments, as well as any third-party or hybrid cloud integrations. This collaborative effort helps ensure that incident response playbooks are aligned with the organization's cloud security posture, compliance requirements, and business objectives. Once the organization's cloud environment has been assessed, incident response teams can begin drafting incident response playbooks that outline specific response procedures and actions for various types of security incidents commonly encountered in cloud environments. These playbooks typically include detailed steps for incident detection, analysis, containment, eradication, recovery, and post-incident review, with each step clearly defined and documented to facilitate consistent and efficient response efforts. For example, an incident response playbook for a cloud-based web application might include procedures for detecting anomalous behavior or suspicious activity in web server logs, analyzing traffic patterns to identify potential attacks or compromises, and containing the incident by isolating affected servers or blocking malicious IP addresses at the network level. CLI commands such as aws cloudtrail create-trail or az monitor diagnostic-settings create can be used to enable cloud logging and monitoring services, capture relevant log data, and configure alerting mechanisms to notify incident response teams of security events or anomalies detected in the cloud environment. Moreover, incident response playbooks should outline communication protocols, escalation procedures, and roles and responsibilities for incident response team members, ensuring clear and effective coordination during incident response activities. This may involve establishing communication channels such as email distribution lists, chat platforms, or incident management tools for real-time collaboration and information sharing among team members, stakeholders, and management personnel. Additionally, incident response playbooks should incorporate incident classification and prioritization criteria to help incident response teams assess the severity and impact of security incidents and allocate resources accordingly. By categorizing incidents based on their potential impact on critical business operations, data confidentiality, integrity, and availability, organizations can prioritize response efforts and focus on mitigating the most significant risks first. Incident response playbooks should also include predefined response actions and decision trees for common scenarios, enabling incident response teams to quickly assess the situation, determine the appropriate course of action, and execute response procedures in a timely manner. This may involve deploying automated response actions or mitigation strategies using cloud-native security tools, scripting languages, or third-party orchestration platforms to streamline incident containment and reduce manual intervention. Additionally, incident response playbooks should be regularly reviewed, updated, and tested to ensure their effectiveness and relevance in addressing emerging threats, evolving attack techniques, and changes in the organization's cloud environment. By conducting tabletop exercises, simulated incident scenarios, or red team-blue team exercises, organizations can validate their incident response playbooks, identify gaps or weaknesses, and refine response procedures to enhance their incident response capabilities. Furthermore, incident response playbooks should be integrated into broader incident management frameworks and processes, aligning with industry best practices, regulatory requirements, and organizational policies for incident response, cybersecurity, and risk management. This integration helps ensure that incident response efforts are coordinated and consistent across the organization, enabling timely and effective response to security incidents in the cloud.

Real-time risk monitoring tools play a pivotal role in the proactive management of security risks and threats in modern digital environments. These tools continuously collect, analyze, and interpret vast amounts of data from various sources to identify potential risks, vulnerabilities, and anomalies in real-time, allowing organizations to promptly detect and respond to emerging security threats. Leveraging advanced analytics, machine learning algorithms, and threat intelligence feeds, real-time risk monitoring tools provide organizations with actionable insights into their security posture, enabling them to make informed decisions and take preventive measures to mitigate risks effectively. These tools monitor diverse data sources, including network traffic, system logs, user activities, application behavior, and external threat feeds, to detect suspicious activities, unauthorized access attempts, malware infections, and other security incidents as they occur. By correlating and contextualizing data from multiple sources, real-time risk monitoring tools can identify patterns, trends, and abnormalities indicative of potential security breaches or compliance violations, allowing organizations to respond swiftly and decisively to mitigate risks and protect their assets. One such tool is Security Information and Event Management (SIEM) platforms, which aggregate, normalize, and analyze log data from various sources across the IT infrastructure to provide real-time visibility into security events and incidents. SIEM platforms use advanced correlation engines and rule-based alerting mechanisms to detect potential security threats and policy violations, generating alerts and notifications for further investigation and remediation. Additionally, SIEM platforms offer dashboards, reports, and customizable analytics capabilities to help organizations gain insights into their security posture, compliance status, and threat landscape, empowering them to proactively manage security risks and strengthen their overall security posture. Another example of a real-time risk monitoring tool is User and Entity Behavior Analytics (UEBA) solutions, which leverage machine learning algorithms to analyze user behavior and identify anomalous activities indicative of insider threats, compromised accounts, or credential misuse. UEBA solutions analyze user logins, file accesses, application usage, and other behavioral patterns to establish baseline behaviors and detect deviations that may indicate potential security risks or malicious activities. By continuously monitoring user behavior and applying advanced analytics, UEBA solutions help organizations detect and respond to insider threats, data breaches, and other security incidents in real-time, enabling them to prevent potential damage and protect sensitive data. Moreover, cloud-native security monitoring and analytics platforms offer real-time visibility and control over cloud infrastructure and services, allowing organizations to monitor and analyze activity logs, configuration changes, and network traffic in cloud environments. These platforms enable organizations to detect and respond to security threats, compliance violations, and operational issues in real-time, providing comprehensive security monitoring and threat detection capabilities tailored to cloud deployments. By integrating with cloud-native APIs and services, these platforms can collect telemetry data from cloud environments, analyze it in real-time, and generate actionable insights and alerts to help organizations identify and mitigate security risks effectively. Additionally, real-time risk monitoring tools often provide integration with incident response orchestration platforms, enabling organizations to automate response actions, trigger remediation workflows, and orchestrate incident response activities based on predefined policies and playbooks. By integrating real-time risk monitoring with incident response orchestration, organizations can streamline their response efforts, accelerate incident resolution, and reduce the impact of security incidents on their operations. In summary, real-time risk monitoring tools play a critical role in helping organizations proactively manage security risks and threats by continuously monitoring, analyzing, and responding to security events and incidents as they occur. By leveraging advanced analytics, machine learning, and automation capabilities, these tools enable organizations to detect, investigate, and mitigate security risks in real-time, empowering them to protect their assets, maintain compliance, and safeguard their reputation in today's evolving threat landscape. Cloud risk reporting metrics are essential tools for organizations to assess and communicate the effectiveness of their cloud security strategies, identify potential vulnerabilities, and prioritize risk mitigation efforts. These metrics provide valuable insights into the current state of cloud security posture, helping organizations make informed decisions to protect their assets and data in cloud environments. One crucial metric is the number of security incidents reported within a given period, which indicates the frequency and severity of security breaches or incidents affecting cloud resources. This metric helps organizations gauge the overall security posture of their cloud infrastructure and identify trends or patterns that may indicate emerging security threats. Another important metric is the mean time to detect (MTTD), which measures the average time taken to detect security incidents or breaches in cloud environments. Organizations strive to minimize MTTD by implementing proactive monitoring and detection mechanisms, such as intrusion detection systems (IDS), security information and event management (SIEM) platforms, and continuous security monitoring solutions. By reducing MTTD, organizations can improve their ability to detect and respond to security incidents promptly, minimizing the potential impact on their operations and data. Additionally, the mean time to respond (MTTR) is a critical metric that measures the average time taken to respond to and mitigate security incidents in cloud environments. Organizations aim to minimize MTTR by establishing incident response processes, workflows, and playbooks, enabling them to respond swiftly and effectively to security incidents as they occur. By reducing MTTR, organizations can limit the damage caused by security incidents and restore normal operations more quickly, minimizing downtime and disruption to their business activities. Moreover, organizations track the number of vulnerabilities identified and remediated in their cloud infrastructure as a key risk reporting metric. Vulnerability management tools and practices play a vital role in identifying and addressing security weaknesses and misconfigurations in cloud environments. Organizations use vulnerability scanning tools to scan cloud resources for known vulnerabilities and assess their severity levels based on industry standards, such as the Common Vulnerability Scoring System (CVSS). They prioritize remediation efforts based on the severity and potential impact of vulnerabilities on their cloud infrastructure and data security. Furthermore, organizations monitor compliance with industry regulations, standards, and best practices as part of their cloud risk reporting metrics. Compliance violations can lead to significant financial penalties, legal liabilities, and reputational damage for organizations operating in regulated industries or handling sensitive data. Therefore, organizations track compliance metrics, such as adherence to data protection regulations (e.g., GDPR, HIPAA), industry-specific security standards (e.g., PCI DSS, ISO 27001), and cloud security best practices (e.g., CIS benchmarks, AWS Well-Architected Framework). They conduct regular audits, assessments, and compliance checks to ensure that their cloud infrastructure and operations meet regulatory requirements and industry standards. Additionally, organizations measure the effectiveness of their security controls and defenses through key performance indicators (KPIs) such as the percentage of security alerts investigated, false positive rates, and the success rate of security incident response and mitigation efforts. These KPIs help organizations evaluate the efficiency and efficacy of their security operations, identify areas for improvement, and optimize their security posture over time. Furthermore, organizations assess the financial impact of security incidents and breaches as part of their cloud risk reporting metrics. They calculate the direct and indirect costs associated with security incidents, including remediation costs, legal expenses, regulatory fines, lost revenue, and damage to brand reputation. By quantifying the financial impact of security incidents, organizations can justify investments in cybersecurity measures, allocate resources effectively, and prioritize risk mitigation efforts based on their potential cost savings and risk reduction benefits. Additionally, organizations track the effectiveness of their security awareness and training programs as part of their cloud risk reporting metrics. Human error and negligence are significant contributors to security incidents and breaches in cloud environments, highlighting the importance of educating employees about security best practices, policies, and procedures. Organizations measure the completion rates, engagement levels, and knowledge retention of their security awareness training programs to assess their effectiveness in improving employees' cybersecurity awareness and behavior. They conduct phishing simulation exercises, security quizzes, and knowledge assessments to evaluate employees' susceptibility to social engineering attacks and identify areas for improvement in their security awareness efforts. In summary, cloud risk reporting metrics are essential for organizations to assess, monitor, and manage security risks in cloud environments effectively. By tracking key metrics related to security incidents, detection and response times, vulnerability management, compliance, security controls effectiveness, financial impact, and security awareness, organizations can gain valuable insights into their cloud security posture, identify areas for improvement, and prioritize risk mitigation efforts to protect their assets and data from cyber threats and breaches.

Risk management in multi-cloud environments is a critical aspect of cloud governance, as organizations increasingly adopt a multi-cloud strategy to leverage the benefits of multiple cloud service providers while mitigating vendor lock-in and enhancing resilience. In multi-cloud environments, organizations face unique challenges and complexities related to risk management, including the need to assess and mitigate risks across different cloud platforms, ensure consistent security controls and policies, and manage dependencies and interconnections between cloud services. One of the key challenges in multi-cloud risk management is maintaining visibility and control over cloud assets, data, and configurations across disparate cloud environments. Organizations often use cloud management platforms (CMPs) and cloud security posture management (CSPM) tools to gain centralized visibility into their multi-cloud infrastructure, monitor for misconfigurations, vulnerabilities, and compliance violations, and enforce security policies consistently across all cloud environments. These tools provide organizations with real-time insights into their cloud security posture, enabling them to identify and remediate security risks proactively. Another challenge in multi-cloud risk management is ensuring data protection and privacy compliance across different jurisdictions and regulatory frameworks. Organizations must navigate complex legal and regulatory requirements when storing, processing, and transmitting data across multiple cloud providers and geographic regions. They employ data encryption, tokenization, and access controls to protect sensitive data and ensure compliance with regulations such as GDPR, HIPAA, and PCI DSS. Additionally, organizations establish data residency and sovereignty policies to specify where data can be stored and processed based on legal and regulatory requirements. Moreover, managing vendor relationships and assessing third-party risks is a critical aspect of multi-cloud risk management. Organizations rely on cloud service providers (CSPs) to deliver essential infrastructure and services, but they must also evaluate the security posture and reliability of their CSPs to ensure they meet their risk management and compliance requirements. Organizations conduct vendor risk assessments, review security certifications and compliance reports, and negotiate service-level agreements (SLAs) with CSPs to establish clear expectations for security, availability, and performance. Furthermore, organizations implement network security controls and segmentation strategies to protect cloud workloads and data from unauthorized access and cyber threats in multi-cloud environments. They deploy virtual private clouds (VPCs), firewalls, intrusion detection and prevention systems (IDPS), and network access control (NAC) solutions to secure network traffic and enforce segmentation between different cloud environments, business units, and user groups. Additionally, organizations leverage cloud-native security services and features provided by cloud providers, such as AWS Security Groups, Azure Virtual Network, and Google Cloud VPC Service Controls, to enforce network security policies and isolate workloads from potential threats. Another aspect of multi-cloud risk management is ensuring business continuity and disaster recovery capabilities across diverse cloud environments. Organizations implement redundant architectures, data replication, and failover mechanisms to minimize the impact of cloud outages, data loss, and service disruptions. They conduct regular disaster recovery testing and simulations to validate the effectiveness of their recovery strategies and ensure they can restore operations quickly in the event of a disaster or service interruption. Moreover, organizations adopt a risk-based approach to multi-cloud governance, prioritizing risk mitigation efforts based on the potential impact and likelihood of security threats and vulnerabilities. They conduct risk assessments, threat modeling, and vulnerability scans to identify and prioritize risks across their multi-cloud infrastructure, applications, and data. Organizations allocate resources and investments based on risk priorities, focusing on high-impact risks that pose the greatest threat to their business objectives and continuity. Additionally, organizations leverage automation and orchestration tools to streamline risk management processes and improve efficiency in multi-cloud environments. They automate security controls deployment, configuration management, vulnerability scanning, and incident response workflows to reduce manual effort, minimize human error, and ensure consistency and accuracy in risk management activities. By integrating security automation into their multi-cloud environments, organizations can enhance their ability to detect, respond to, and mitigate security risks rapidly and effectively. In summary, risk management in multi-cloud environments is a complex and multifaceted discipline that requires organizations to adopt a holistic approach to identify, assess, and mitigate risks effectively. By leveraging cloud management tools, implementing robust security controls and policies, managing vendor relationships, securing network connections, ensuring business continuity, and prioritizing risk mitigation efforts based on business priorities and risk profiles, organizations can enhance the security, resilience, and compliance of their multi-cloud deployments.

Advanced threat intelligence and risk forecasting play crucial roles in modern cybersecurity strategies, providing organizations with proactive insights into emerging threats and vulnerabilities that could impact their digital assets and operations. Threat intelligence encompasses the collection, analysis, and dissemination of information about potential cyber threats, including indicators of compromise (IOCs), tactics, techniques, and procedures (TTPs) used by threat actors, and contextual information about the motives and capabilities of adversaries. By leveraging threat intelligence feeds, organizations can enhance their ability to detect and respond to cyber threats in real-time, enabling them to prevent security incidents and minimize their impact on business operations. One of the key components of threat intelligence is the identification and analysis of IOCs, which are artifacts or observables associated with malicious activities, such as IP addresses, domain names, file hashes, and email addresses. Organizations use threat intelligence platforms (TIPs) and security information and event management (SIEM) systems to ingest and correlate IOCs from various sources, including open-source threat feeds, commercial intelligence providers, and internal security telemetry. By correlating IOCs with security events and logs from across the enterprise, organizations can identify potential security incidents and prioritize their response efforts based on the severity and relevance of the threats. Moreover, threat intelligence analysis involves identifying patterns and trends in cyber threats, such as common attack vectors, targeted industries, and emerging malware families. Security analysts leverage data analytics and machine learning algorithms to analyze large volumes of threat data and identify correlations and anomalies that could indicate malicious activity. By understanding the tactics and techniques used by threat actors, organizations can anticipate their adversaries' behavior and proactively adjust their security controls and policies to mitigate the risk of successful attacks. Additionally, threat intelligence provides organizations with contextual information about the motives and objectives of threat actors, enabling them to assess the potential impact and likelihood of specific cyber threats. By understanding the motivations behind cyber attacks, organizations can tailor their security defenses and response strategies to effectively counter the tactics employed by adversaries. For example, if threat intelligence indicates that a threat actor is motivated by financial gain, organizations may prioritize monitoring for indicators of fraud or data exfiltration and implement controls to protect sensitive financial information. Furthermore, risk forecasting involves predicting future cyber threats and vulnerabilities based on historical data, industry trends, and threat intelligence analysis. Organizations use predictive analytics and modeling techniques to assess the likelihood and potential impact of various cyber risks, such as data breaches, ransomware attacks, and supply chain compromises. By quantifying the probability and severity of potential security incidents, organizations can allocate resources and investments more effectively to mitigate their exposure to cyber threats. For example, if risk forecasting indicates an increased likelihood of phishing attacks targeting employee credentials, organizations may invest in security awareness training programs and multi-factor authentication (MFA) solutions to strengthen their defenses against credential theft. Additionally, risk forecasting enables organizations to prioritize risk mitigation efforts based on their potential impact on business objectives and continuity. By identifying high-risk areas and vulnerabilities in advance, organizations can implement proactive measures to reduce their exposure to cyber threats and minimize the likelihood of security incidents occurring. Moreover, organizations can use risk forecasting to inform strategic decision-making and resource allocation, such as determining budget allocations for cybersecurity initiatives, selecting security controls and technologies, and defining incident response priorities. By integrating threat intelligence and risk forecasting into their cybersecurity programs, organizations can enhance their ability to detect, assess, and mitigate cyber threats effectively, enabling them to protect their digital assets, maintain business continuity, and safeguard their reputation and customer trust.

BOOK 4
MASTERING CLOUD SECURITY
EXPERT INSIGHTS AND BEST PRACTICES FOR CCSP
CERTIFICATION

ROB BOTWRIGHT

Emerging threat vectors in cloud computing pose significant challenges to the security posture of organizations as they adopt cloud services and infrastructure to support their digital transformation initiatives. One such threat vector is serverless computing, which introduces new attack surfaces and potential vulnerabilities due to its event-driven architecture and reliance on third-party cloud services. Attackers can exploit misconfigurations in serverless functions or inject malicious code into event triggers to execute arbitrary commands or exfiltrate sensitive data from cloud environments. To mitigate these risks, organizations must implement security best practices for serverless deployments, such as enforcing least privilege access controls, implementing function-level authentication and authorization mechanisms, and regularly scanning serverless code for vulnerabilities using static and dynamic analysis tools. Another emerging threat vector is container orchestration platforms, such as Kubernetes, which are increasingly targeted by attackers seeking to exploit misconfigurations and vulnerabilities in containerized applications and infrastructure. Attackers can compromise Kubernetes clusters to launch distributed denial-of-service (DDoS) attacks, execute cryptojacking campaigns, or exfiltrate sensitive data stored in container volumes. Organizations can enhance the security of their Kubernetes deployments by following security best practices, such as restricting access to the Kubernetes API server, enabling network policies to control traffic between pods, and regularly applying security patches and updates to the underlying infrastructure. Additionally, organizations should implement container image scanning and signing solutions to identify and mitigate vulnerabilities in container images before they are deployed to production environments. Furthermore, edge computing introduces new threat vectors and security challenges as organizations extend their IT infrastructure to the network edge to support latency-sensitive applications and IoT devices. Attackers can exploit vulnerabilities in edge computing platforms and devices to launch distributed denial-of-service (DDoS) attacks, intercept sensitive data transmitted over unsecured networks, or compromise edge nodes to gain unauthorized access to corporate networks and resources. To address these risks, organizations must implement security controls and monitoring mechanisms at the network edge, such as firewalls, intrusion detection systems (IDS), and security information and event management (SIEM) solutions, to detect and respond to malicious activities in real-time. Additionally, organizations should encrypt data transmitted between edge devices and cloud-based services using secure protocols and cryptographic algorithms to protect it from unauthorized interception and tampering. Moreover, the adoption of artificial intelligence (AI) and machine learning (ML) technologies introduces new threat vectors and attack opportunities as attackers leverage AI-powered tools and techniques to evade detection and bypass traditional security defenses. For example, attackers can use adversarial machine learning techniques to generate malicious inputs that exploit vulnerabilities in AI models or manipulate training data to produce biased or inaccurate predictions. To mitigate these risks, organizations must implement robust security controls and monitoring mechanisms for AI and ML systems, such as data validation and sanitization routines, model explainability and interpretability techniques, and adversarial robustness testing frameworks. Additionally, organizations should establish threat hunting and incident response capabilities to detect and respond to AI-driven attacks in real-time, enabling them to identify and mitigate security incidents before they escalate into full-blown breaches. Furthermore, the proliferation of Internet of Things (IoT) devices introduces new threat vectors and attack surfaces as organizations deploy interconnected devices to monitor and control physical assets and infrastructure. Attackers can exploit vulnerabilities in IoT devices to launch botnet attacks, compromise sensitive data stored on device endpoints, or gain unauthorized access to corporate networks and systems. To address these risks, organizations must implement security best practices for IoT deployments, such as securing device firmware and software updates, enforcing strong authentication and access controls, and segmenting IoT networks from corporate IT environments to minimize the impact of potential compromises. Additionally, organizations should deploy IoT security solutions, such as intrusion detection and prevention systems (IDPS), network traffic analysis tools, and device management platforms, to detect and respond to security threats in real-time, enabling them to protect their IoT deployments from malicious actors and unauthorized activities. In summary, emerging threat vectors in cloud computing pose significant challenges to organizations as they strive to secure their digital assets and infrastructure in an increasingly interconnected and dynamic environment. By implementing robust security controls and monitoring mechanisms, adopting security best practices for emerging technologies, and establishing threat detection and response capabilities, organizations can enhance their ability to detect, prevent, and mitigate cyber threats effectively, enabling them to safeguard their data, applications, and operations from malicious actors and security breaches.

Advanced Persistent Threats (APTs) pose a significant risk to organizations operating in cloud environments, leveraging sophisticated techniques and strategies to infiltrate and compromise sensitive data and *resources. APTs are typically orchestrated by well-funded and highly skilled threat actors, including nation-state-sponsored groups, criminal organizations, and hacktivist collectives, aiming to achieve long-term access to targeted systems and networks. These adversaries employ a variety of tactics, techniques, and procedures (TTPs) to evade detection, circumvent security controls, and maintain persistence within compromised environments. One common tactic used by APT actors is reconnaissance, wherein they gather intelligence about their target's infrastructure, applications, and personnel to identify vulnerabilities and weaknesses that can be exploited to gain unauthorized access. This often involves scanning for open ports, enumerating system services, and conducting social engineering attacks to gather credentials and other sensitive information. Once initial access is established, APT actors deploy advanced malware and exploit kits to compromise additional systems and escalate privileges within the target environment. They may exploit known vulnerabilities in software and operating systems or employ zero-day exploits to bypass security defenses and gain unauthorized access to critical systems and data. To maintain persistence and evade detection, APT actors often use stealthy techniques, such as fileless malware, rootkit implants, and custom-built backdoors that blend into legitimate system processes and traffic. These techniques enable APT actors to maintain a foothold in compromised environments for* extended periods, allowing them to exfiltrate sensitive data, steal intellectual property, or disrupt critical operations without being detected. To detect and mitigate APTs in cloud environments, organizations must implement robust security controls and monitoring mechanisms capable of detecting and responding to suspicious activities and anomalous behavior in real-time. This includes deploying endpoint detection and response (EDR) solutions, network intrusion detection systems (NIDS), and security information and event management (SIEM) platforms to collect, correlate, and analyze security telemetry from across the cloud infrastructure. Additionally, organizations should conduct regular threat hunting exercises to proactively search for signs of compromise and malicious activity within their environment, enabling them to identify and neutralize APTs before they can cause significant harm. Furthermore, organizations must prioritize employee training and awareness programs to educate personnel about the risks associated with APTs and teach them how to recognize and respond to suspicious emails, attachments, and other indicators of compromise. By promoting a culture of security awareness and vigilance, organizations can empower their employees to act as the first line of defense against APTs and other cyber threats. Additionally, organizations should implement robust access controls and least privilege principles to limit the impact of potential APT attacks and prevent lateral *movement within their cloud environments. This includes enforcing strong authentication mechanisms, implementing network segmentation, and regularly reviewing and updating access permissions to ensure that only authorized users have access to sensitive data and resources. Furthermore, organizations should leverage threat intelligence feeds and information sharing platforms to stay abreast of emerging APT campaigns, tactics, and techniques, enabling them to adapt their security strategies and defenses accordingly. By collaborating with industry peers, security vendors, and government agencies, organizations can enhance their ability to detect and mitigate APTs effectively, minimizing the risk of data breaches, financial losses, and reputational damage. In summary, APTs represent a significant and evolving threat to organizations operating in cloud environments, posing a range of risks and challenges that must be addressed through proactive security measures, robust monitoring capabilities, and continuous threat intelligence sharing. By implementing a comprehensive security strategy that incorporates advanced detection and response capabilities, employee training and awareness initiatives, and collaboration with industry partners, organizations can enhance their resilience to APTs and protect their data, applications, and infrastructure from malicious actors and sophisticated cyber threats.*

Cloud Security Reference Architectures provide comprehensive blueprints for designing and implementing robust security controls and mechanisms within cloud environments, offering organizations a structured approach to securing their data, applications, and infrastructure. These architectures are based on industry best practices, regulatory requirements, and security standards, providing organizations with a framework for building secure and resilient cloud deployments that meet their specific business needs and compliance obligations. One widely recognized Cloud Security Reference Architecture is the Cloud Security Alliance (CSA) Cloud Controls Matrix (CCM), which defines a set of security controls and guidelines for assessing the security posture of cloud service providers and evaluating their suitability for hosting sensitive workloads and data. The CCM is organized into 16 control domains, covering areas such as data security, identity and access management, encryption, and incident response, providing organizations with a comprehensive framework for evaluating and implementing security controls within their cloud environments. Another popular

Cloud Security Reference Architecture is the National Institute of Standards and Technology (NIST) Special Publication 800-53, which provides a catalog of security controls and guidelines for securing federal information systems and infrastructure. NIST SP 800-53 covers a wide range of security domains, including access control, risk management, security assessment and authorization, and security operations, offering organizations a flexible and scalable framework for building secure cloud deployments that align with their risk management objectives and regulatory requirements. Additionally, cloud service providers such as Amazon Web Services (AWS), Microsoft Azure, and Google Cloud Platform (GCP) offer their own Cloud Security Reference Architectures and best practice guides for securing their respective cloud services and platforms. These reference architectures provide organizations with prescriptive guidance on configuring security features and controls within their cloud environments, helping them leverage the built-in security capabilities of cloud service providers to protect their data and workloads from unauthorized access, data breaches, and other security threats. For example, AWS offers the AWS Well-Architected Framework, which provides a set of best practices and design principles for building secure, high-performing, and resilient cloud architectures. The Well-Architected

Framework covers areas such as operational excellence, security, reliability, performance efficiency, and cost optimization, offering organizations a holistic approach to designing and deploying secure cloud solutions that align with their business objectives and security requirements. Similarly, Microsoft Azure provides the Azure Security Benchmark, which offers a set of security controls and recommendations for securing Azure resources and workloads. The Azure Security Benchmark covers areas such as identity and access management, network security, data protection, and threat detection and response, helping organizations implement effective security measures within their Azure environments to mitigate risks and protect their assets from cyber threats. Likewise, Google Cloud Platform offers the Google Cloud Security Foundations Framework, which provides a set of security controls and best practices for securing Google Cloud services and infrastructure. The Security Foundations Framework covers areas such as identity and access management, data protection, network security, and compliance, offering organizations a structured approach to implementing security controls and mechanisms within their Google Cloud deployments. In summary, Cloud Security Reference Architectures play a critical role in helping organizations design and implement secure cloud deployments, providing *them with prescriptive guidance, best practices, and security controls for protecting their data, applications, and infrastructure from cyber threats. By leveraging industry-standard frameworks such as the CSA CCM, NIST SP 800-53, and cloud service provider-specific reference architectures, organizations can build secure, compliant, and resilient cloud environments that meet their security requirements and support their business objectives. Secure design patterns for cloud services are essential blueprints that provide guidance on how to architect and implement secure cloud-based solutions to protect against various cyber threats and security vulnerabilities. These design patterns offer organizations a structured approach to designing and deploying cloud services that prioritize security and compliance requirements, ensuring the confidentiality, integrity, and availability of their data and applications. One common secure design pattern is the Zero Trust Architecture, which assumes that no entity, whether inside or outside the network, should be trusted by default and requires strict authentication and authorization mechanisms for accessing resources. Implementing the Zero Trust Architecture involves deploying identity and access management (IAM) solutions such as AWS Identity and Access Management (IAM), Azure Active Directory (AD), or Google Cloud Identity and Access Management*

(IAM) to manage user identities and enforce granular access controls based on roles, permissions, and attributes. Additionally, organizations can leverage multi-factor authentication (MFA) solutions such as AWS Multi-Factor Authentication (MFA), Azure Multi-Factor Authentication (MFA), or Google Authenticator to add an extra layer of security and prevent unauthorized access to their cloud resources. Another secure design pattern is the Defense in Depth approach, which involves implementing multiple layers of security controls and mechanisms to create overlapping layers of defense and minimize the risk of a successful cyber attack. Deploying the Defense in Depth approach requires organizations to implement a combination of network security, host-based security, application security, and data security controls to protect their cloud services from various attack vectors. For example, organizations can use AWS Web Application Firewall (WAF), Azure Application Gateway Firewall, or Google Cloud Armor to protect their web applications from common web-based attacks such as SQL injection, cross-site scripting (XSS), and cross-site request forgery (CSRF). Additionally, organizations can deploy intrusion detection and prevention systems (IDS/IPS) such as AWS GuardDuty, Azure Security Center, or Google Cloud Security Command Center to monitor and

analyze network traffic for suspicious activity and automatically block malicious traffic in real-time. Furthermore, organizations can leverage cloud-native security services such as AWS Security Hub, Azure Security Center, or Google Cloud Security Command Center to gain visibility into their cloud environments, identify security misconfigurations and vulnerabilities, and remediate security issues proactively. Another secure design pattern is the Immutable Infrastructure approach, which involves treating infrastructure as code and deploying new instances of infrastructure rather than modifying existing ones. This approach helps organizations minimize the risk of configuration drift and enforce consistent security configurations across their cloud environments. Implementing the Immutable Infrastructure approach requires organizations to use infrastructure as code (IaC) tools such as AWS CloudFormation, Azure Resource Manager (ARM), or Google Cloud Deployment Manager to define and provision cloud resources using code templates. Additionally, organizations can leverage configuration management tools such as AWS Systems Manager, Azure Automation, or Google Cloud Config Management to enforce security baselines and compliance standards on their cloud resources automatically. Furthermore, organizations can implement continuous integration and continuous deployment (CI/CD) pipelines using tools such as AWS CodePipeline, Azure DevOps, or Google Cloud Build to automate the deployment and testing of infrastructure changes and ensure that only approved and validated changes are deployed to production environments. Additionally, organizations can leverage cloud-native encryption services such as AWS Key Management Service (KMS), Azure Key Vault, or Google Cloud Key Management Service (KMS) to encrypt data at rest and in transit and protect sensitive information from unauthorized access. Another secure design pattern is the Data Loss Prevention (DLP) approach, which involves implementing controls and mechanisms to prevent the unauthorized disclosure of sensitive data and protect against data breaches. Deploying the DLP approach requires organizations to classify their data based on sensitivity and apply encryption, access controls, and data masking techniques to protect sensitive information from unauthorized access and disclosure. For example, organizations can use AWS Macie, Azure Information Protection, or Google Cloud Data Loss Prevention (DLP) to automatically classify and label sensitive data, monitor data access and usage, and enforce data protection policies based on predefined rules and conditions. Additionally, organizations can implement data encryption techniques such as AWS S3 Server-Side Encryption (SSE), Azure Storage Service Encryption (SSE), or Google Cloud Storage

Encryption to encrypt data at rest and protect it from unauthorized access. Furthermore, organizations can use data masking techniques such as tokenization, redaction, and anonymization to obfuscate sensitive information in non-production environments and minimize the risk of data exposure during development and testing activities. In summary, secure design patterns for cloud services provide organizations with a set of proven strategies and best practices for designing and deploying secure and resilient cloud-based solutions. By implementing secure design patterns such as Zero Trust Architecture, Defense in Depth, Immutable Infrastructure, and Data Loss Prevention, organizations can strengthen their security posture, mitigate the risk of cyber attacks and data breaches, and ensure the confidentiality, integrity, and availability of their data and applications in the cloud.

Securing public cloud deployments is a critical aspect of modern IT infrastructure management, requiring a comprehensive understanding of security best practices and the implementation of robust security controls to protect sensitive data and applications from cyber threats. One fundamental aspect of securing public cloud deployments is ensuring that proper access controls are in place to restrict unauthorized access to resources and data stored in the cloud environment. This involves configuring identity and access management (IAM) policies to define granular permissions and roles for users, groups, and applications. For example, in AWS, IAM policies can be defined using the AWS Management Console, AWS Command Line Interface (CLI), or AWS Software Development Kits (SDKs) to grant specific permissions to users or roles. Similarly, in Azure, Azure Active Directory (AD) can be used to manage user identities and enforce access controls to Azure resources using role-based access control (RBAC) policies. Additionally, in Google Cloud Platform (GCP), Identity and Access Management (IAM) roles can be assigned to users and service accounts to control access to GCP resources. Another crucial aspect of securing public cloud deployments is implementing network security controls to protect against external threats and unauthorized access. This involves configuring virtual private clouds (VPCs), subnets, and network security groups (NSGs) to control inbound and outbound traffic to and from cloud resources. For example, in AWS, VPCs can be configured using the AWS Management Console or AWS CLI to define network boundaries and security groups to control traffic flow. Similarly, in Azure, Virtual Networks (VNets) can be configured using the Azure portal or Azure CLI to isolate resources and enforce network security policies using NSGs. Moreover, in GCP, Virtual Private Clouds (VPCs) can be created and managed using the Google Cloud Console or gcloud command-line tool to define firewall rules and control traffic between resources. Securing data in transit and at rest is also critical for public cloud deployments, as it helps prevent unauthorized access and data breaches. This involves implementing encryption techniques to protect data both during transmission over the network and while stored in cloud storage services. For example, in AWS, data can be encrypted using AWS Key Management Service (KMS) to manage encryption keys and encrypt data at rest in Amazon S3 buckets or Amazon EBS volumes. Similarly, in Azure, Azure Storage Service Encryption (SSE) can be used to automatically encrypt data at rest in Azure Blob

Storage or Azure Disk Storage. Additionally, in GCP, Google Cloud Key Management Service (KMS) can be used to encrypt data at rest in Google Cloud Storage (GCS) or Google Compute Engine (GCE) disks. Furthermore, securing public cloud deployments involves implementing security monitoring and logging solutions to detect and respond to security incidents in real-time. This includes configuring cloud-native monitoring services such as AWS CloudWatch, Azure Monitor, or Google Cloud Monitoring to collect and analyze logs, metrics, and events from cloud resources. Additionally, organizations can deploy third-party security information and event management (SIEM) solutions such as Splunk, Elastic Security, or Sumo Logic to aggregate and correlate security data from multiple sources and provide centralized visibility into security events. Moreover, organizations can leverage cloud-native threat detection and response services such as AWS GuardDuty, Azure Security Center, or Google Cloud Security Command Center to automatically detect and respond to security threats and anomalies in the cloud environment. Furthermore, securing public cloud deployments involves implementing security best practices for containerized workloads to protect against container escapes, privilege escalation, and other container-specific threats. This includes configuring container orchestration platforms such as Amazon

Elastic Kubernetes Service (EKS), Azure Kubernetes Service (AKS), or Google Kubernetes Engine (GKE) to enforce security policies and limit access to sensitive resources. Additionally, organizations can implement container security solutions such as AWS Container Security, Azure Container Registry, or Google Container Registry to scan container images for vulnerabilities and enforce security policies at runtime. Moreover, organizations can leverage container runtime security tools such as Aqua Security, Sysdig Secure, or Twistlock to monitor container activity, detect anomalous behavior, and prevent malicious activities in real-time. In summary, securing public cloud deployments requires a proactive and multi-layered approach to address various security challenges and protect against evolving cyber threats. By implementing robust access controls, network security measures, data encryption techniques, security monitoring solutions, and container security best practices, organizations can strengthen their cloud security posture and mitigate the risk of security breaches and data loss in the public cloud environment. Best practices for private cloud security encompass a range of strategies and techniques aimed at safeguarding the confidentiality, integrity, and availability of data and applications hosted within a private cloud environment. One fundamental aspect of private cloud security is establishing robust access controls to limit unauthorized access to sensitive resources and data. This involves implementing role-based access control (RBAC) policies to assign granular permissions to users, groups, and applications based on their roles and responsibilities within the organization. For example, in VMware vSphere, access control can be managed using vCenter Server's Role-Based Access Control (RBAC) feature, which allows administrators to create custom roles and assign permissions to users and groups. Similarly, in OpenStack, access control can be enforced using the Keystone identity service, which supports RBAC and allows administrators to define access policies for different types of users. Additionally, in Microsoft Hyper-V, access control can be managed using Active Directory (AD) security groups and permissions to restrict access to virtual machines and other resources. Another essential aspect of private cloud security is implementing strong network segmentation to isolate sensitive workloads and data from unauthorized access. This involves dividing the private cloud environment into separate network segments or VLANs and enforcing strict firewall rules to control traffic flow between them. For example, in VMware NSX, network segmentation can be achieved using logical switches and distributed firewall rules to create micro-segmentation zones and restrict lateral movement of threats within the private cloud environment.

Similarly, in OpenStack, network segmentation can be enforced using Neutron's network segmentation features, such as security groups and VLANs, to isolate workloads and enforce traffic filtering rules. Moreover, in Microsoft Hyper-V, network segmentation can be achieved using Hyper-V Network Virtualization (HNV) to create isolated virtual networks and enforce firewall policies using Windows Firewall with Advanced Security. Additionally, private cloud security involves implementing encryption techniques to protect data both at rest and in transit. This includes encrypting sensitive data stored in virtual machines, databases, and storage volumes using strong encryption algorithms and cryptographic keys. For example, in VMware vSphere, data encryption can be enabled using vSphere VM Encryption to encrypt virtual machine disks and ensure data confidentiality. Similarly, in OpenStack, data encryption can be achieved using encryption technologies such as LUKS (Linux Unified Key Setup) to encrypt virtual machine disks and Swift encryption to encrypt data stored in object storage. Additionally, in Microsoft Hyper-V, data encryption can be implemented using BitLocker Drive Encryption to encrypt virtual machine disks and ensure data protection. Moreover, private cloud security involves implementing robust security monitoring and logging solutions to detect and respond to security incidents in real-time. This includes deploying intrusion detection and prevention systems (IDPS), security information and event management (SIEM) solutions, and log management platforms to collect, analyze, and correlate security data from various sources within the private cloud environment. For example, in VMware vSphere, security monitoring can be achieved using vRealize Log Insight to collect and analyze logs from virtual machines, hosts, and other components. Similarly, in OpenStack, security monitoring can be implemented using third-party SIEM solutions such as Splunk or ELK (Elasticsearch, Logstash, Kibana) to aggregate and analyze security events from different OpenStack services. Additionally, in Microsoft Hyper-V, security monitoring can be achieved using Windows Event Log and Microsoft System Center Operations Manager (SCOM) to monitor and alert on security-related events. Furthermore, private cloud security involves implementing regular security assessments and audits to identify and remediate security vulnerabilities and compliance gaps. This includes conducting vulnerability scans, penetration testing, and security audits to assess the effectiveness of security controls and ensure compliance with industry regulations and standards. For example, in VMware vSphere, security assessments can be performed using vRealize Operations Manager to analyze the security posture of virtual infrastructure and identify potential security risks. Similarly, in OpenStack, security assessments can be conducted using third-party vulnerability scanning tools such as Nessus or Qualys to identify security vulnerabilities in OpenStack deployments. Additionally, in Microsoft Hyper-V, security assessments can be performed using Microsoft Baseline Security Analyzer (MBSA) to scan virtual machines and hosts for security misconfigurations and vulnerabilities. In summary, implementing best practices for private cloud security is essential for safeguarding sensitive data and applications hosted within a private cloud environment. By establishing robust access controls, implementing network segmentation, encrypting data, deploying security monitoring solutions, and conducting regular security assessments, organizations can strengthen their private cloud security posture and mitigate the risk of security breaches and data loss.

Homomorphic encryption is a groundbreaking cryptographic technique that enables computations to be performed on encrypted data without decrypting it first, thereby preserving privacy and confidentiality in cloud computing environments. This technique holds immense promise for securely outsourcing data processing tasks to untrusted cloud service providers while ensuring that sensitive data remains protected from unauthorized access. One of the key advantages of homomorphic encryption is its ability to support various types of computations on encrypted data, including addition, multiplication, and more complex operations, without revealing the underlying plaintext. This is achieved through the use of mathematical operations that preserve the structure of the encrypted data, allowing computations to be performed directly on ciphertexts. For example, suppose a user wants to compute the sum of two encrypted numbers stored in the cloud. Instead of decrypting the numbers first, performing the addition operation, and then encrypting the result again, homomorphic encryption allows the addition operation to be performed directly on the encrypted numbers, yielding an encrypted result that can be decrypted to obtain the sum of the plaintext numbers.

This enables secure and privacy-preserving data processing in scenarios where sensitive data needs to be outsourced to the cloud for computation while maintaining confidentiality. One of the most widely studied and used forms of homomorphic encryption is the partially homomorphic encryption scheme, which supports either addition or multiplication operations on encrypted data but not both. However, recent advancements in cryptography have led to the development of fully homomorphic encryption (FHE) schemes, which support arbitrary computations on encrypted data, including both addition and multiplication operations. FHE schemes are more complex and computationally intensive than partially homomorphic encryption schemes but offer greater flexibility and functionality for secure cloud computing applications. Implementing homomorphic encryption in cloud environments requires careful consideration of various factors, including the choice of encryption scheme, key management practices, and performance overhead. One popular homomorphic encryption library that facilitates the implementation of homomorphic encryption in cloud environments is the Microsoft Simple Encrypted Arithmetic Library (SEAL), which provides efficient implementations of both partially and fully homomorphic encryption schemes. Using SEAL, developers can perform computations on encrypted data using a high-level programming interface and integrate homomorphic encryption into their cloud applications with ease. Additionally, several cloud service providers offer homomorphic encryption as a service, allowing users to perform secure computations on encrypted data without the need to manage encryption keys or infrastructure. For example, Microsoft Azure provides a fully managed homomorphic encryption service called Microsoft Azure Confidential Computing, which enables users to perform computations on encrypted data in a secure and privacy-preserving manner. To deploy homomorphic encryption in a cloud environment using Microsoft Azure Confidential Computing, users can leverage the Azure SDK for Python to interact with the homomorphic encryption service and perform computations on encrypted data. This involves creating a secure enclave within the Azure cloud environment, uploading encrypted data to the enclave, and executing computations on the encrypted data using homomorphic encryption techniques. The result of the computation is then securely returned to the user without exposing the underlying plaintext data to the cloud service provider. Similarly, other cloud service providers offer homomorphic encryption capabilities as part of their cloud offerings, allowing users to perform secure computations on encrypted data in a scalable and cost-effective manner. In summary, homomorphic encryption is a powerful cryptographic technique that enables secure and privacy-preserving data processing in cloud computing environments. By allowing computations to be performed directly on encrypted data, homomorphic encryption mitigates the risk of data breaches and unauthorized access while enabling the outsourcing of data processing tasks to untrusted cloud service providers. With advancements in cryptography and the availability of cloud-based homomorphic encryption services, organizations can leverage this technology to enhance the security and privacy of their cloud-based applications and services.

Post-quantum cryptography considerations have become increasingly important in recent years due to the potential threat posed by quantum computers to traditional cryptographic algorithms. With the rapid advancement of quantum computing technology, there is a growing concern that quantum computers could break existing cryptographic schemes, compromising the security of sensitive data and communications. As a result, researchers and cryptographic experts have been working to develop new cryptographic algorithms that are resistant to attacks from quantum computers, a field known as post-quantum cryptography. One of the main challenges in post-quantum cryptography is designing algorithms that can withstand attacks from both classical and quantum computers while maintaining efficiency and security. Many of the cryptographic algorithms currently in use, such as RSA and ECC, rely on mathematical problems that are believed to be hard to solve using classical computers but can be efficiently solved using quantum algorithms, such as

Shor's algorithm. To address this vulnerability, researchers have been exploring alternative mathematical problems and structures that are believed to be resistant to attacks from quantum computers. One approach is to use lattice-based cryptography, which relies on the hardness of certain lattice problems to provide security. Lattice-based cryptography offers strong security guarantees and is considered one of the most promising candidates for post-quantum cryptography. Another approach is to use hash-based cryptography, which relies on the properties of cryptographic hash functions to provide security. Hash-based cryptography has a long history of use and is well-understood, making it an attractive option for post-quantum cryptography. Other approaches to post-quantum cryptography include code-based cryptography, multivariate polynomial cryptography, and isogeny-based cryptography, each of which relies on different mathematical structures and problems to provide security. Deploying post-quantum cryptography in practice requires careful consideration of various factors, including algorithm performance, compatibility with existing systems, and the potential impact on security. Many organizations are beginning to evaluate post-quantum cryptographic algorithms and develop transition plans to migrate to post-quantum secure systems. One important consideration in deploying post-quantum cryptography is the need for interoperability with existing cryptographic systems and protocols.

Transitioning to post-quantum secure systems will require updating cryptographic protocols and algorithms across a wide range of systems and applications, which may take time and effort. Additionally, organizations will need to ensure that post-quantum cryptographic algorithms are efficiently implemented and supported in hardware and software implementations. This may require collaboration with vendors and industry partners to develop and deploy post-quantum secure systems. Another consideration is the potential impact of post-quantum cryptography on system performance and resource usage. Some post-quantum cryptographic algorithms are computationally intensive and may require more computational resources to achieve the same level of security as traditional cryptographic algorithms. Organizations will need to carefully evaluate the performance characteristics of post-quantum cryptographic algorithms and consider their impact on system performance and scalability. Additionally, organizations will need to consider the potential legal and regulatory implications of deploying post-quantum cryptography. As post-quantum cryptographic algorithms are relatively new and may not yet be standardized or widely adopted, organizations may need to navigate legal and regulatory requirements related to the use of cryptographic algorithms in their jurisdiction. This may involve consulting with legal experts and regulatory authorities to ensure compliance with applicable laws and regulations. Despite these challenges, post-quantum cryptography offers a promising solution to the threat posed by quantum computers to traditional cryptographic algorithms. By developing and deploying post-quantum secure systems, organizations can ensure the long-term security of their sensitive data and communications in an increasingly quantum-enabled world.

Secure coding practices for cloud applications are essential to ensure the confidentiality, integrity, and availability of data and services in cloud environments. One fundamental aspect of secure coding in the cloud is adhering to the principle of least privilege, which means granting users and processes only the permissions necessary to perform their tasks. This principle helps minimize the potential impact of security breaches by limiting the access that attackers have to sensitive resources. In cloud environments, implementing least privilege often involves using access control mechanisms such as Role-Based Access Control (RBAC) or Attribute-Based Access Control (ABAC) to enforce fine-grained access policies. For example, in Amazon Web Services (AWS), you can use AWS Identity and Access Management (IAM) to define roles and policies that specify which actions users and resources are allowed to perform. Similarly, in Microsoft Azure, you can use Azure Role-Based Access Control (RBAC) to assign roles to users and resources to control their access to Azure resources.

Another important aspect of secure coding in the cloud is validating and sanitizing input to prevent common security vulnerabilities such as injection attacks. Injection attacks, such as SQL injection and cross-site scripting (XSS), occur when an attacker is able to inject malicious code or commands into an application's input, which can then be executed by the application. To prevent injection attacks, developers should use parameterized queries and input validation techniques to ensure that input data is properly sanitized before being used in queries or executed by the application. For example, in a web application running on AWS, you can use AWS WAF (Web Application Firewall) to filter and monitor HTTP requests for common attack patterns, such as SQL injection and XSS attacks.

Additionally, secure coding practices for cloud applications should include implementing strong encryption and cryptographic protocols to protect sensitive data both in transit and at rest. This involves using industry-standard encryption algorithms and key management practices to securely store and transmit data. For example, in Google Cloud Platform (GCP), you can use Cloud Key Management Service (KMS) to manage cryptographic keys and encrypt data at rest using the Advanced Encryption Standard (AES). Similarly, in Azure, you can use Azure Key Vault to store and manage cryptographic keys, secrets, and certificates used by cloud applications.

Furthermore, secure coding practices for cloud applications should address the importance of secure authentication and session management to prevent unauthorized access to sensitive resources. This involves implementing strong authentication mechanisms, such as multi-factor authentication

(MFA), and securely managing user sessions to prevent session hijacking and other attacks. For example, in AWS, you can use AWS Identity and Access Management (IAM) to enforce MFA for IAM users, or you can use Amazon Cognito to add user sign-up, sign-in, and access control to your web and mobile apps.

Moreover, secure coding practices for cloud applications should include regular security testing and vulnerability scanning to identify and remediate security issues before they can be exploited by attackers. This involves conducting regular security assessments, such as penetration testing and code reviews, to identify vulnerabilities and weaknesses in the application's code and configuration. Additionally, developers should use automated tools and services, such as AWS Inspector or Azure Security Center, to continuously monitor and analyze the security posture of their cloud applications and infrastructure.

In summary, adopting secure coding practices for cloud applications is essential to protect against evolving security threats and ensure the security and integrity of data and services in cloud environments. By following best practices such as implementing least privilege, validating input, using strong encryption, and conducting regular security testing, developers can build and deploy secure cloud applications that meet the highest standards of security and compliance.

Integrating security into Continuous Integration/Continuous Deployment (CI/CD) pipelines is crucial for ensuring that software applications are developed and deployed securely throughout their lifecycle. One of the key aspects of integrating security into CI/CD pipelines is the use of automated security testing tools and techniques to identify and remediate vulnerabilities early in the development process. For example, developers can use static application security testing (SAST) tools such as SonarQube or Checkmarx to scan the source code for common security issues such as code injection vulnerabilities or insecure coding practices. Similarly, dynamic application security testing (DAST) tools like OWASP ZAP or Burp Suite can be used to test running applications for vulnerabilities such as cross-site scripting (XSS) or SQL injection.

Moreover, integrating security into CI/CD pipelines involves implementing security gates or checkpoints at various stages of the pipeline to ensure that only code that meets predefined security criteria is allowed to proceed to the next stage of deployment. For example, developers can configure automated security scans to run as part of the CI/CD pipeline, and if any critical vulnerabilities are identified, the pipeline can be halted until the issues are addressed. This helps prevent insecure code from being deployed to production environments and reduces the risk of security breaches.

Additionally, integrating security into CI/CD pipelines requires collaboration between development, operations, and security teams to ensure that security considerations are taken into account at every stage of the pipeline. This can involve incorporating security requirements into the definition of user stories or tasks, conducting security reviews of code changes before they are merged into the main codebase, and performing regular security assessments of the pipeline itself to identify and mitigate potential security risks.

Furthermore, integrating security into CI/CD pipelines involves ensuring that security controls are applied consistently across all environments, including development, testing, and production. This can be achieved by using infrastructure as code (IaC) tools such as Terraform or AWS CloudFormation to define and provision cloud resources in a consistent and repeatable manner. By codifying security controls as part of the infrastructure definition, developers can ensure that security measures such as network segmentation, encryption, and access control are applied consistently across all environments.

Moreover, integrating security into CI/CD pipelines requires implementing secure deployment practices to minimize the risk of security breaches during the deployment process. This can involve using containerization technologies such as Docker or Kubernetes to package applications and their dependencies into portable containers, which can then be deployed consistently across different environments. Additionally, developers can use deployment automation tools such as Jenkins or GitLab CI/CD to automate the deployment process and ensure that security controls such as access control and encryption are applied consistently.

Furthermore, integrating security into CI/CD pipelines involves monitoring and logging to detect and respond to security incidents in real-time. This can involve implementing centralized logging and monitoring solutions such as ELK Stack or Splunk to collect and analyze logs from various sources, including applications, infrastructure, and network devices. Additionally, developers can use security information and event management (SIEM) tools such as AWS GuardDuty or Azure Sentinel to detect and respond to security threats in real-time.

In summary, integrating security into CI/CD pipelines is essential for ensuring that software applications are developed and deployed securely. By incorporating automated security testing, implementing security gates, collaborating across teams, applying security controls consistently, implementing secure deployment practices, and monitoring and logging, organizations can build and deploy secure software applications that meet the highest standards of security and compliance.

Cloud-native security controls are essential for protecting applications and data in cloud environments, where traditional security approaches may not be sufficient. These controls are specifically designed to address the unique security challenges posed by cloud-native architectures, which often involve microservices, containers, serverless computing, and other cloud-native technologies. One of the key cloud-native security controls is identity and access management (IAM), which governs who can access what resources within a cloud environment. IAM controls can be enforced using identity providers such as AWS Identity and Access Management (IAM) or Google Cloud Identity and Access Management (IAM), which allow organizations to define fine-grained access policies based on roles, groups, and permissions. These policies can then be enforced using IAM roles or service accounts, which grant users or applications access to specific resources based on their assigned permissions.

Another important cloud-native security control is network security, which involves securing communication between different components of a cloud-native application. This can be achieved using network security groups (NSGs) or virtual private clouds (VPCs), which allow organizations to define network access controls based on IP addresses, ports, and protocols. Additionally, organizations can use network segmentation techniques such as micro-segmentation to isolate workloads and limit the blast radius of security incidents. For example, AWS provides security groups and network ACLs (Access Control Lists) to control inbound and outbound traffic at the instance and subnet level, while Azure offers network security groups (NSGs) to filter network traffic based on rules.

Moreover, container security is a critical aspect of cloud-native security, given the widespread adoption of containerization technologies such as Docker and Kubernetes. Container security controls include image scanning, runtime protection, and access control. Image scanning involves scanning container images for vulnerabilities and misconfigurations before they are deployed to production environments. Tools such as Docker Security Scanning or Clair can be used to automatically scan container images for known vulnerabilities and provide actionable insights to developers. Furthermore, runtime protection involves monitoring and securing containers while they are running in production environments. This can be achieved using tools such as Kubernetes Network Policies or Istio Service Mesh, which allow organizations to define and enforce fine-grained access controls between different microservices running within a Kubernetes cluster.

In addition to container security, serverless security is also a key concern in cloud-native environments. Serverless computing platforms such as AWS Lambda or Google Cloud Functions allow developers to run code without managing underlying infrastructure, but they also introduce new security challenges. Serverless security controls include access control, function monitoring, and resource isolation. Access control involves defining and enforcing permissions for serverless functions using IAM roles or function policies. Function monitoring involves monitoring the execution of serverless functions for security anomalies or suspicious behavior. Tools such as AWS CloudTrail or Google Cloud Audit Logs can be used to track function invocations and detect security incidents in real-time. Furthermore, resource isolation involves ensuring that serverless functions are isolated from each other and from other resources within the cloud environment. This can be achieved using techniques such as AWS Lambda VPC, which allows organizations to run serverless functions within their own virtual private cloud (VPC) and control network access using security groups and network ACLs.

Furthermore, data security is a critical aspect of cloud-native security, given the importance of protecting sensitive data in cloud environments. Data security controls include encryption, data masking, and data loss prevention (DLP). Encryption involves encrypting data both at rest and in transit to protect it from unauthorized access. Cloud providers such as AWS and

Azure offer native encryption services such as AWS Key Management Service (KMS) or Azure Key Vault, which allow organizations to encrypt data using encryption keys managed by the cloud provider. Data masking involves obscuring sensitive data to prevent unauthorized access. This can be achieved using techniques such as tokenization or data anonymization, which replace sensitive data with non-sensitive placeholders. Additionally, data loss prevention (DLP) involves monitoring and controlling the movement of sensitive data within a cloud environment to prevent unauthorized disclosure. Tools such as AWS Macie or Google Cloud DLP can be used to automatically identify and classify sensitive data and enforce data protection policies based on predefined rules.

In summary, cloud-native security controls are essential for protecting applications and data in cloud environments. These controls encompass a wide range of security measures, including identity and access management, network security, container security, serverless security, and data security. By implementing these controls, organizations can mitigate the risks associated with cloud-native architectures and build secure and compliant cloud-native applications.

Advanced endpoint security solutions play a critical role in protecting cloud workloads from a wide range of cyber threats and vulnerabilities, ensuring the security and integrity of data stored and processed in cloud environments. These solutions leverage innovative technologies and methodologies to detect, prevent, and respond to security incidents at the endpoint level, offering comprehensive protection against malware, ransomware, phishing attacks, and other sophisticated cyber threats. One such advanced endpoint security solution is endpoint detection and response (EDR), which provides real-time monitoring, threat hunting, and incident response capabilities to detect and neutralize advanced threats across cloud workloads. EDR solutions continuously monitor endpoint activities and behaviors, analyzing them for signs of malicious activity or anomalous behavior that may indicate a security breach.

Deploying an EDR solution involves installing lightweight agents on each endpoint within the cloud environment and configuring them to collect and analyze telemetry data such as process executions, file modifications, network connections, and system events. Once deployed, the EDR solution can identify and investigate suspicious activities, generate alerts for potential security incidents, and facilitate rapid response and remediation actions to contain and mitigate threats. For example, a security analyst can use the EDR console to investigate a suspicious process execution by querying historical telemetry data, analyzing process memory dumps, or conducting forensic investigations to determine the root cause of the incident.

Another advanced endpoint security solution is endpoint protection platforms (EPP), which offer a broad set of security capabilities to defend against known and unknown threats, including antivirus, antimalware, firewall, intrusion prevention, and behavioral analysis. EPP solutions use advanced detection techniques such as machine learning, artificial intelligence, and behavioral analysis to identify and block malicious activities in real-time, providing proactive defense against evolving threats. Deploying an EPP solution involves installing security agents on endpoints and configuring them to enforce security policies and controls based on the organization's security requirements and compliance standards.

Furthermore, cloud workload protection platforms (CWPP) offer comprehensive security capabilities specifically designed for cloud-native workloads, including virtual machines, containers, and serverless functions. CWPP solutions provide visibility, control, and protection across the entire cloud workload lifecycle, from development and deployment to runtime and decommissioning. These platforms integrate with cloud-native orchestration tools such as Kubernetes and AWS Lambda to automatically discover and secure cloud workloads, enforce security policies, and detect and respond to security threats in real-time. For example, a CWPP solution can automatically deploy security agents or sidecar containers to monitor and protect containerized workloads, enforce network segmentation policies, and detect and block malicious activities.

Moreover, cloud access security brokers (CASB) provide advanced security controls and visibility into cloud-based applications and services, allowing organizations to enforce data protection policies, detect and remediate security threats, and ensure compliance with regulatory requirements. CASB solutions offer features such as data loss prevention (DLP), cloud access controls, threat intelligence, and user behavior analytics to secure cloud workloads and prevent unauthorized access, data leakage, and insider threats. Deploying a CASB solution involves integrating it with cloud-based applications and services through APIs or proxy agents, configuring security policies and controls, and monitoring and analyzing user activities and data transactions for security violations.

Additionally, next-generation antivirus (NGAV) solutions leverage advanced detection techniques such as behavioral analysis, machine learning, and threat intelligence to identify and block sophisticated malware and ransomware threats targeting cloud workloads. NGAV solutions provide multi-layered protection against known and unknown threats, offering real-time visibility, threat detection, and automated response capabilities to defend against evolving cyber threats. Deploying an NGAV solution involves installing lightweight agents on endpoints and configuring them to communicate with a centralized management console for policy enforcement, threat detection, and incident response.

In summary, advanced endpoint security solutions play a crucial role in protecting cloud workloads from a wide range of cyber threats and vulnerabilities. These solutions leverage innovative technologies and methodologies to detect, prevent, and respond to security incidents in real-time, offering comprehensive protection against malware, ransomware, phishing attacks, and other sophisticated threats. By deploying advanced endpoint security solutions, organizations can enhance the security and integrity of their cloud workloads, safeguarding sensitive data and ensuring compliance with regulatory requirements.

Advanced security incident response frameworks are essential components of cybersecurity strategies, providing organizations with structured methodologies and processes to detect, respond to, and recover from security incidents effectively. These frameworks go beyond traditional incident response approaches by integrating advanced technologies, threat intelligence, and automation to enhance incident detection, analysis, and response capabilities. One such framework is the NIST Computer Security Incident Handling Guide, which provides organizations with a comprehensive approach to managing and responding to security incidents. The NIST framework consists of four key phases: preparation, detection and analysis, containment, eradication, and recovery, and post-incident activity. Each phase includes specific activities and tasks designed to help organizations effectively respond to security incidents and minimize their impact on business operations.

To deploy the NIST incident response framework, organizations can use various tools and technologies to automate and streamline incident detection, analysis, and response processes. For example, organizations can use Security Information and Event Management (SIEM) systems to collect, correlate, and analyze security event data from across the enterprise, enabling them to detect and respond to security incidents in real-time. Additionally, organizations can leverage Threat Intelligence Platforms (TIPs) to gather and analyze threat intelligence data from external sources, such as threat feeds, forums, and dark web sources, to identify emerging threats and vulnerabilities that may pose a risk to their environment.

Another advanced security incident response framework is the Cyber Kill Chain model, which provides organizations with a systematic approach to understanding and countering cyber threats. The Cyber Kill Chain model consists of seven stages: reconnaissance, weaponization, delivery, exploitation, installation, command and control, and actions on objectives. By understanding each stage of the attack lifecycle, organizations can develop proactive defenses and countermeasures to disrupt and thwart cyber attacks before they can cause harm. To deploy the Cyber Kill Chain framework, organizations can use threat intelligence feeds, network monitoring tools, and endpoint detection and response (EDR) solutions to detect and respond to threats at each stage of the attack lifecycle.

Furthermore, the MITRE ATT&CK framework is a valuable resource for organizations looking to improve their security incident response capabilities. The MITRE ATT&CK framework provides a comprehensive matrix of adversary tactics, techniques, and procedures (TTPs) organized into various categories, such as initial access, execution, persistence, and exfiltration. By mapping known TTPs to specific stages of the attack lifecycle, organizations can identify gaps in their security defenses and develop effective countermeasures to detect, prevent, and respond to cyber threats. To deploy the MITRE ATT&CK framework, organizations can use threat intelligence feeds, security analytics platforms, and endpoint detection and response (EDR) solutions to map observed TTPs to the MITRE ATT&CK matrix and identify potential security gaps and weaknesses.

Moreover, organizations can leverage Incident Response Orchestration Platforms (IROPs) to automate and streamline incident response processes, enabling them to respond to security incidents more efficiently and effectively. IROPs provide organizations with centralized consoles and workflows to coordinate and automate incident response activities, such as alert triage, investigation, containment, and remediation. By integrating with existing security tools and technologies, such as SIEM systems, EDR solutions, and threat intelligence feeds, IROPs can orchestrate and automate incident response actions across the enterprise, helping organizations reduce response times and mitigate the impact of security incidents.

Additionally, organizations can use Security Orchestration, Automation, and Response (SOAR) platforms to integrate and automate security operations and incident response processes. SOAR platforms provide organizations with capabilities to orchestrate and automate security workflows, such as incident triage, investigation, containment, and remediation, across disparate security tools and technologies. By leveraging playbooks and workflows, organizations can standardize and streamline incident response processes, enabling them to respond to security incidents more effectively and efficiently. To deploy a SOAR platform, organizations can integrate it with existing security tools and technologies, such as SIEM systems, EDR solutions, and threat intelligence feeds, to automate incident response actions and improve overall security posture.

In summary, advanced security incident response frameworks play a crucial role in helping organizations detect, respond to, and recover from security incidents effectively. By leveraging structured methodologies, advanced technologies, and automation capabilities, organizations can enhance their incident response capabilities and minimize the impact of security incidents on business operations. Deploying advanced incident response frameworks involves leveraging tools and technologies such as SIEM systems, threat intelligence platforms, EDR solutions, IROPs, and SOAR platforms to automate and streamline incident detection, analysis, and response processes. By integrating these tools and technologies into their security operations, organizations can improve their ability to detect, respond to, and recover from security incidents in a timely and efficient manner.

Threat hunting and security analytics are critical components of cybersecurity strategies in cloud environments, enabling organizations to proactively identify and mitigate potential threats and vulnerabilities. Threat hunting involves the proactive search for malicious activity or security breaches within an organization's network or cloud infrastructure, while security analytics focuses on the analysis of security data to identify patterns, trends, and anomalies that may indicate a security threat. Together, these approaches provide organizations with the visibility and insights needed to detect and respond to security incidents before they can cause harm.

To effectively hunt for threats and analyze security data in cloud environments, organizations can leverage a combination of tools, technologies, and methodologies. One such tool is a Security Information and Event Management (SIEM) system, which collects and correlates security event data from various sources, such as network devices, servers, and cloud services. SIEM systems use advanced analytics and machine learning algorithms to identify suspicious behavior and security incidents, enabling organizations to respond quickly and effectively. To deploy a SIEM system in a cloud environment, organizations can use cloud-native SIEM solutions that are specifically designed to integrate with cloud platforms and services, such as Amazon Web Services (AWS), Microsoft Azure, and Google Cloud Platform (GCP).

Additionally, organizations can use Endpoint Detection and Response (EDR) solutions to hunt for threats and analyze security data on individual endpoints, such as laptops, desktops, and servers. EDR solutions provide organizations with real-time visibility into endpoint activity and behavior, enabling them to detect and respond to advanced threats and malware. To deploy an EDR solution in a cloud environment, organizations can deploy lightweight agents on their virtual machines and containers to monitor endpoint activity and collect security data. These agents can then send security data to a centralized management console or SIEM system for analysis and correlation.

Advanced penetration testing techniques are crucial for evaluating the security posture of cloud infrastructures, ensuring that they can withstand sophisticated cyber threats. These techniques go beyond traditional penetration testing approaches, incorporating advanced methodologies, tools, and tactics to identify vulnerabilities and weaknesses in cloud environments. One such technique is the use of automated vulnerability scanners, such as OpenVAS or Nessus, to perform comprehensive vulnerability assessments of cloud infrastructures. These scanners can identify known vulnerabilities in cloud-based systems, services, and applications, enabling organizations to prioritize and remediate security issues effectively.

Another advanced penetration testing technique is the use of cloud-specific exploitation frameworks, such as CloudSploit or CloudGoat, to simulate real-world attacks against cloud infrastructures. These frameworks provide pre-configured attack scenarios and payloads designed to exploit common misconfigurations and vulnerabilities in cloud environments. By simulating attacks against their own cloud infrastructures, organizations can identify and remediate security weaknesses before they can be exploited by malicious actors.

Additionally, organizations can leverage cloud-specific enumeration and reconnaissance tools, such as AWS CLI or GCP CLI, to gather information about cloud resources, configurations, and permissions. These tools allow penetration testers to identify potential attack vectors, such as exposed storage buckets or misconfigured access controls, that could be exploited to gain unauthorized access to sensitive data or resources in the cloud.

Furthermore, advanced penetration testing techniques may involve the use of custom-built attack tools and scripts to bypass security controls and evade detection mechanisms in cloud environments. For example, penetration testers may develop custom payloads or exploits to target specific vulnerabilities or weaknesses in cloud-based applications or services. By using custom-built tools and techniques, penetration testers can assess the effectiveness of security controls and defenses in cloud infrastructures under realistic attack scenarios.

Moreover, organizations can perform advanced penetration testing exercises, such as red team engagements or adversary simulation exercises, to assess their ability to detect and respond to sophisticated cyber threats in cloud environments. These exercises involve emulating the tactics, techniques, and procedures (TTPs) of real-world threat actors to assess the effectiveness of security controls and incident response capabilities in cloud infrastructures. By simulating realistic attack scenarios, organizations can identify gaps in their security defenses and develop effective mitigation strategies to improve their overall security posture.

In addition to technical testing techniques, organizations can also conduct social engineering and phishing campaigns to assess the human element of security in cloud environments. These campaigns involve sending simulated phishing emails or conducting social engineering attacks against employees to test their awareness of security threats and their ability to identify and report suspicious activities. By raising awareness and providing security training to employees, organizations can reduce the risk of successful phishing attacks and improve overall security awareness in cloud environments.

Furthermore, organizations can leverage threat intelligence feeds and threat hunting techniques to proactively identify and mitigate security threats in cloud environments. Threat intelligence feeds provide organizations with real-time information about emerging threats, vulnerabilities, and attack patterns, enabling them to detect and respond to security incidents more effectively. Threat hunting involves actively searching for signs of malicious activity or unauthorized access in cloud infrastructures using advanced analytics and machine learning techniques. By combining threat intelligence with threat hunting capabilities, organizations can enhance their ability to detect and respond to sophisticated cyber threats in cloud environments.

Additionally, organizations can implement continuous security monitoring and logging solutions to collect, analyze, and correlate security event data from cloud environments in real-time. Solutions such as AWS CloudTrail or Azure Monitor allow organizations to monitor user activity, resource changes, and network traffic in cloud infrastructures, enabling them to detect and respond to security incidents as they occur. By implementing continuous security monitoring, organizations can gain visibility into their cloud environments and detect potential security threats before they can cause significant harm.

In summary, advanced penetration testing techniques are essential for evaluating and improving the security posture of cloud infrastructures. By leveraging automated vulnerability scanners, cloud-specific exploitation frameworks, enumeration and reconnaissance tools, custom-built attack tools, red team engagements, social engineering and phishing campaigns, threat intelligence feeds, threat hunting techniques, and continuous security monitoring solutions, organizations can assess their security defenses and identify vulnerabilities and weaknesses in cloud environments. By identifying and mitigating security threats proactively, organizations can strengthen their security posture and protect their sensitive data and resources in the cloud.

Automated security testing tools are invaluable assets for evaluating the security posture of cloud environments, providing organizations with the ability to identify vulnerabilities, misconfigurations, and compliance issues efficiently and effectively. These tools streamline the security testing process, enabling organizations to conduct comprehensive assessments of their cloud infrastructures in a timely manner. One such tool is Amazon Inspector, a service that automatically assesses the security and compliance of AWS environments, providing detailed findings and recommendations for remediation. By running assessments on EC2 instances, Amazon Inspector helps organizations identify security vulnerabilities and compliance violations, such as exposed ports, outdated software, and missing patches, allowing them to address these issues proactively.

Another popular automated security testing tool for cloud environments is Nessus, a vulnerability scanner that enables organizations to scan their *cloud infrastructures for known vulnerabilities and misconfigurations. By leveraging Nessus, organizations can identify security weaknesses in their cloud-based systems and services, such as insecure network configurations, weak authentication mechanisms, and outdated software versions, helping them prioritize and remediate security issues effectively.*

Additionally, organizations can use tools like Qualys Cloud Platform to perform continuous security assessments of their cloud environments, enabling them to monitor and manage security risks in real-time. Qualys Cloud Platform provides organizations with a centralized dashboard for monitoring the security posture of their cloud infrastructures, allowing them to track vulnerabilities, compliance violations, and security incidents across multiple cloud providers and regions.

Furthermore, organizations can leverage open-source security testing tools, such as OWASP ZAP (Zed Attack Proxy) or OpenSCAP (Security Content Automation Protocol), to assess the security of their cloud-based applications and services. OWASP ZAP is a widely-used penetration testing tool that helps organizations identify and exploit vulnerabilities in web applications hosted in cloud environments, such as SQL injection, cross-site scripting (XSS), and insecure direct object references (IDORs). OpenSCAP, on the other hand, is a security compliance scanning tool that enables organizations to evaluate the security configuration of their cloud-based systems against industry-standard security baselines, such as CIS benchmarks and NIST guidelines.

Moreover, organizations can use container security scanning tools, such as Clair or Trivy, to assess the security of container images deployed in cloud environments. These tools analyze container images for known vulnerabilities and misconfigurations, providing organizations with actionable insights to improve the security of their containerized workloads. By integrating container security scanning into their CI/CD pipelines, organizations can ensure that only secure and compliant container images are deployed to production environments.

Additionally, organizations can leverage cloud-native security services, such as Azure Security Center or Google Cloud Security Command Center, to automate security testing and compliance monitoring in their cloud environments. These services provide organizations with centralized visibility into their cloud infrastructures, enabling them to identify security risks, detect security threats, and enforce compliance policies across their cloud workloads.

Furthermore, organizations can use Infrastructure as Code (IaC) security scanning tools, such as Checkov or Terraform Compliance, to assess the security of their cloud infrastructure configurations. These tools analyze IaC templates and configuration files for security best practices, compliance violations, and misconfigurations, helping organizations identify and remediate security issues early in the development lifecycle.

In summary, automated security testing tools play a crucial role in ensuring the security and compliance of cloud environments. By leveraging tools like Amazon Inspector, Nessus, Qualys Cloud Platform, OWASP ZAP, OpenSCAP, container security scanning tools, cloud-native security services, and IaC security scanning tools, organizations can automate security assessments, detect vulnerabilities and misconfigurations, and enforce compliance policies effectively. By integrating automated security testing into their DevSecOps workflows, organizations can improve the overall security posture of their cloud infrastructures and mitigate security risks proactively.

Automated security policy enforcement in cloud environments is a critical aspect of maintaining the integrity and security of digital assets deployed in cloud infrastructure. With the increasing complexity and scale of cloud deployments, manual enforcement of security policies becomes impractical, necessitating the use of automated tools and processes to ensure compliance with security standards and regulations. One such approach to automated security policy enforcement is leveraging cloud-native security services provided by leading cloud service providers like AWS, Azure, and Google Cloud. These services offer a range of features and capabilities for enforcing security policies across various layers of the cloud stack, including identity and access management (IAM), network security, data protection, and threat detection.

For example, AWS Identity and Access Management (IAM) enables organizations to define granular access control policies that govern user and application access to AWS resources. By using IAM policies, organizations can enforce least privilege access principles, ensuring that users and applications have only the permissions necessary to perform their intended tasks. IAM policies can be defined using

JSON syntax and attached to IAM users, groups, or roles using the AWS Management Console, AWS CLI, or AWS SDKs.

Similarly, Azure Policy is a service in Microsoft Azure that helps organizations enforce compliance with corporate standards and regulatory requirements across their Azure environments. Azure Policy allows organizations to define policy rules that specify the desired configuration settings for Azure resources, such as virtual machines, storage accounts, and databases. These policy rules can be written in JSON format and enforced using Azure Policy assignments, which are applied at the subscription, resource group, or resource level.

Google Cloud Platform (GCP) offers a similar capability called Organization Policy, which enables organizations to define and enforce policies across their GCP environments. Organization Policy allows organizations to create custom policies that govern resource configuration, access controls, and security settings. These policies can be written in YAML or JSON format and applied to GCP projects using the Google Cloud Console, gcloud command-line tool, or Google Cloud APIs.

In addition to cloud-native security services, organizations can use third-party security automation tools and platforms to enforce security policies in cloud environments. These tools provide advanced capabilities for automating security policy enforcement workflows, such as continuous *compliance monitoring, policy remediation, and security incident response. For example, HashiCorp Terraform is a popular infrastructure as code (IaC) tool that enables organizations to define infrastructure configurations using code and enforce security policies through automated deployment pipelines. With Terraform, organizations can define security policies as code using the HashiCorp Configuration Language (HCL) and apply them to cloud resources using Terraform plans and deployments.*

Furthermore, organizations can leverage cloud security posture management (CSPM) platforms, such as Palo Alto Networks Prisma Cloud and CloudGuard from Check Point Software, to enforce security policies across multi-cloud environments. These platforms provide centralized visibility into cloud assets and configurations, enabling organizations to assess security risks, detect policy violations, and enforce security controls across their cloud estates. By integrating CSPM platforms into their cloud security workflows, organizations can automate policy enforcement tasks and ensure continuous compliance with security standards and regulations.

Overall, automated security policy enforcement is essential for maintaining the security and compliance of cloud environments in today's digital landscape. By leveraging cloud-native security services, third-party automation tools, and CSPM platforms, organizations can enforce security policies effectively, mitigate security risks, and protect their critical assets from cyber threats. With the increasing adoption of cloud computing, automated security policy enforcement will continue to play a vital role in safeguarding cloud-based infrastructure and data assets against evolving security threats and regulatory requirements.

Cloud Compliance as Code (CaC) techniques represent a paradigm shift in the way organizations manage and enforce compliance requirements in cloud environments, offering a streamlined and automated approach to ensuring adherence to security standards and regulatory frameworks. At its core, CaC leverages infrastructure as code (IaC) principles to define and deploy compliance policies as code, enabling organizations to codify their compliance requirements and integrate them into their DevOps pipelines. This approach provides several benefits, including increased agility, consistency, and scalability in managing compliance across distributed and dynamic cloud infrastructures.

One of the key components of Cloud Compliance as Code is the use of declarative configuration files to define compliance policies in a machine-readable format. These configuration files, typically written in YAML or JSON, specify the desired state of cloud resources and the rules and controls that must be enforced to maintain compliance. For example, organizations can use tools like AWS CloudFormation or Terraform to define infrastructure configurations and security policies using code, which can then be deployed and managed alongside application code.

Using Terraform as an example, organizations can define compliance policies using Terraform configuration files, known as Terraform scripts or templates. These scripts describe the desired state of cloud resources, including their configuration settings, access controls, and security policies. For instance, organizations can use Terraform to define policies that enforce encryption of data at rest for all storage resources, such as Amazon S3 buckets or Azure Blob Storage containers. This can be achieved by specifying encryption settings in the Terraform configuration file and applying the changes using the terraform apply command.

Similarly, organizations can use tools like AWS Config or Azure Policy to define and enforce compliance rules across their cloud environments. AWS Config allows organizations to create rules that automatically assess the configuration of AWS resources against predefined compliance standards, such as the CIS AWS Foundations Benchmark or the AWS Well-Architected Framework. These rules can be created using the AWS Management Console or the AWS CLI and applied to specific AWS accounts or resources using AWS Config rules.

In Azure, organizations can use Azure Policy to define and enforce compliance policies for Azure resources. Azure Policy enables organizations to create policy definitions that specify the desired configuration settings for Azure resources, such as virtual machines, databases, and networking components. These policy definitions can be authored using JSON or Azure Resource Manager (ARM) templates and applied to Azure subscriptions or resource groups using Azure Policy assignments.

Another important aspect of Cloud Compliance as Code is the integration of compliance checks into continuous integration and continuous deployment (CI/CD) pipelines. By incorporating compliance checks into CI/CD workflows, organizations can ensure that compliance requirements are validated automatically during the application development and deployment process. For example, organizations can use tools like AWS CodePipeline or Azure DevOps to define CI/CD pipelines that include automated compliance checks using AWS Config rules or Azure Policy.

Moreover, Cloud Compliance as Code enables organizations to achieve continuous compliance monitoring and enforcement by automating the assessment and remediation of compliance violations. For instance, organizations can use AWS Config rules or Azure Policy to detect non-compliant resources in real-time and trigger automated remediation actions, such as sending notifications or rolling back changes. By automating compliance monitoring and enforcement, organizations can reduce the risk of security breaches and ensure that their cloud environments remain compliant with regulatory requirements.

Overall, Cloud Compliance as Code represents a fundamental shift in how organizations approach compliance management in cloud environments, offering a more agile, scalable, and automated approach to ensuring adherence to security standards and regulatory frameworks. By leveraging infrastructure as code principles, declarative configuration files, and integration with CI/CD pipelines, organizations can achieve greater efficiency and effectiveness in managing compliance across their cloud infrastructures. As organizations continue to embrace cloud computing, Cloud Compliance as Code will play an increasingly important role in enabling them to meet their compliance obligations while maintaining agility and innovation in their cloud deployments.

Cloud Security Orchestration and Automation Platforms (SOAPs) are sophisticated tools designed to streamline and enhance security operations in cloud environments by automating repetitive tasks, orchestrating complex workflows, and integrating with various security tools and technologies. These platforms play a crucial role in helping organizations improve their security posture, respond more effectively to security incidents, and mitigate emerging threats in the rapidly evolving landscape of cloud computing.

SOAPs offer a wide range of capabilities to address different aspects of cloud security, including threat detection, incident response, compliance management, and vulnerability management. One of the key features of SOAPs is their ability to automate repetitive security tasks, such as log analysis, threat intelligence aggregation, and malware detection, which can help reduce the workload on security teams and enable them to focus on more strategic activities. For example, organizations can use SOAPs to automatically ingest security logs from various cloud services, analyze them for suspicious activity using predefined rules and machine learning algorithms, and generate alerts or notifications for potential security incidents.

Moreover, SOAPs enable organizations to orchestrate complex security workflows across multiple tools and technologies, allowing them to automate end-to-end security processes and workflows. This orchestration capability is particularly valuable in cloud environments where organizations may use a variety of security tools and services from different vendors. By integrating these tools and services into a unified workflow, SOAPs can help organizations improve visibility, coordination, and collaboration across their security operations. For instance, organizations can use SOAPs to automate incident response workflows, such as triaging alerts, investigating security incidents, and coordinating remediation actions across different teams and departments.

Furthermore, SOAPs provide advanced capabilities for integrating with third-party security tools and technologies, enabling organizations to leverage their existing investments in security infrastructure and extend the functionality of their SOAPs. These integrations allow organizations to centralize security data and workflows, streamline their security operations, and improve their overall security posture. For example, SOAPs can integrate with threat intelligence platforms to enrich security alerts with additional context and prioritize them based on their relevance and severity.

Additionally, SOAPs offer comprehensive capabilities for managing compliance requirements in cloud environments, including regulatory compliance frameworks such as GDPR, HIPAA, and PCI DSS. SOAPs can automate compliance assessments, generate compliance reports, and provide real-time visibility into compliance status across cloud environments. This helps organizations ensure that they are meeting their compliance obligations and reduce the risk of regulatory fines and penalties. For example, SOAPs can automatically scan cloud environments for misconfigurations, vulnerabilities, and policy violations, and remediate them according to predefined compliance standards.

Furthermore, SOAPs provide robust capabilities for managing vulnerabilities in cloud environments, including vulnerability scanning, prioritization, and remediation. SOAPs can automatically discover and inventory assets in cloud environments, scan them for known vulnerabilities using vulnerability databases and threat feeds, and prioritize vulnerabilities based on their severity and exploitability. This helps organizations identify and address security weaknesses before they can be exploited by attackers, reducing the risk of security breaches and data loss.

Moreover, SOAPs offer advanced analytics and reporting capabilities, allowing organizations to gain insights into their security posture, identify emerging threats and trends, and measure the effectiveness of their security controls. SOAPs can collect and analyze security data from various sources, including logs, events, and alerts, and provide customizable dashboards and reports to visualize key security metrics and KPIs. This helps organizations make informed decisions about their security investments and prioritize their security efforts based on their risk profile and business objectives.

Additionally, SOAPs provide robust capabilities for incident response and threat hunting in cloud environments, enabling organizations to detect and respond to security incidents in real-time. SOAPs can automatically correlate security events and alerts from different sources, such as intrusion detection systems, firewalls, and endpoint protection platforms, and orchestrate response actions based on predefined playbooks and workflows. This helps organizations minimize the impact of security incidents, contain the spread of threats, and recover from security breaches more quickly and efficiently.

Furthermore, SOAPs offer advanced capabilities for threat intelligence management and sharing, allowing organizations to collect, analyze, and disseminate threat intelligence data from various sources, such as open-source feeds, commercial providers, and industry groups. SOAPs can automatically ingest threat intelligence feeds, enrich security alerts with contextual information, and share actionable intelligence with other security tools and platforms. This helps organizations stay ahead of emerging threats, identify new attack vectors, and proactively defend against cyber threats in cloud environments.

In summary, Cloud Security Orchestration and Automation Platforms (SOAPs) are powerful tools that play a critical role in helping organizations improve their security posture, respond more effectively to security incidents, and mitigate emerging threats in cloud environments. By automating repetitive tasks, orchestrating complex workflows, integrating with third-party security tools, and providing advanced analytics and reporting capabilities, SOAPs enable organizations to enhance their security operations, reduce risk, and achieve compliance in the dynamic and challenging landscape of cloud computing.

Zero Trust Architecture (ZTA) is a security concept based on the principle of "never trust, always verify," which assumes that threats could be both outside and inside the network perimeter, and thus, trust should not be granted implicitly to users, devices, or applications, even if they are within the corporate network or cloud environment. Implementing Zero Trust Architecture in cloud environments involves a comprehensive approach to security that focuses on securing access to resources based on identity, device posture, and other contextual factors, rather than relying solely on network-based controls. One of the key components of Zero Trust Architecture is identity and access management (IAM), which involves verifying the identity of users and devices and granting access to resources based on least privilege principles. In a cloud environment, IAM controls are typically implemented using a combination of identity providers, such as Azure Active Directory or AWS Identity and Access Management (IAM), and cloud-native authentication and authorization mechanisms, such as OAuth and JSON Web Tokens (JWT). These controls enable organizations to enforce strong authentication methods, such as multi-factor authentication (MFA) and conditional access policies, to verify the identity of users and devices before granting access to cloud resources.

Another important aspect of Zero Trust Architecture is network segmentation, which involves dividing the network into smaller, isolated segments or microsegments to contain the impact of security incidents and limit lateral movement by attackers. In cloud environments, network segmentation can be achieved using virtual private clouds (VPCs), security groups, and network access control lists (ACLs) to restrict traffic between different tiers of applications and enforce least privilege access controls. For example, organizations can use VPC peering and private connectivity options, such as AWS Direct Connect or Azure ExpressRoute, to establish secure connections between on-premises data centers and cloud environments, while limiting access to specific IP addresses or subnets.

Additionally, Zero Trust Architecture emphasizes the importance of continuous monitoring and analytics to *detect and respond to security threats in real-time. In a cloud environment, organizations can leverage cloud-native security services, such as AWS GuardDuty or Azure Security Center, to monitor and analyze network traffic, user behavior, and system logs for signs of suspicious activity or security incidents. These services use machine learning algorithms and threat intelligence feeds to identify potential security threats, such as malware infections, unauthorized access attempts, or data exfiltration attempts, and generate alerts or notifications for security teams to investigate further.*

Furthermore, Zero Trust Architecture promotes the use of encryption and data protection mechanisms to safeguard sensitive information and prevent unauthorized access or disclosure. In a cloud environment, organizations can use encryption techniques, such as SSL/TLS encryption for data in transit and encryption at rest for data stored in cloud databases or object storage services, to protect data from eavesdropping and unauthorized access. Additionally, organizations can implement data loss prevention (DLP) policies and access controls to prevent sensitive data from being shared or leaked unintentionally.

Moreover, Zero Trust Architecture encourages organizations to adopt a holistic approach to security that encompasses people, processes, and technology. This includes implementing security policies and procedures that govern how users access and use cloud resources, conducting regular security training and awareness programs to educate employees about security best practices and potential threats, and establishing incident response and recovery plans to mitigate the impact of security incidents and ensure business continuity. By integrating security into every aspect of the organization's operations and culture, organizations can create a strong security posture that is resilient to emerging threats and evolving attack vectors.

Additionally, Zero Trust Architecture promotes the use of automation and orchestration to streamline security operations and reduce the time and effort required to detect and respond to security threats. In a cloud environment, organizations can use automation tools, such as AWS Lambda or Azure Functions, to automate routine security tasks, such as patch management, vulnerability scanning, and incident response, and orchestration platforms, such as AWS Step Functions or Azure Logic Apps, to coordinate and execute complex security workflows across different cloud services and environments. These automation and orchestration capabilities enable organizations to respond more quickly and effectively to security incidents, minimize manual errors, and improve overall operational efficiency.

Furthermore, Zero Trust Architecture emphasizes the importance of collaboration and information sharing between different stakeholders, including security teams, IT operations teams, and business units. By breaking down silos and fostering a culture of collaboration and shared responsibility, organizations can improve their ability to detect and respond to security threats effectively. This includes establishing cross-functional incident response teams, conducting regular security reviews and assessments, and sharing threat intelligence and best practices with other organizations and industry partners.

In summary, implementing Zero Trust Architecture in cloud environments requires a comprehensive approach to security that encompasses identity and access management, network segmentation, continuous monitoring and analytics, encryption and data protection, automation and orchestration, and collaboration and information sharing. By adopting a Zero Trust mindset and implementing these key principles and best practices, organizations can strengthen their security posture, reduce the risk of security breaches, and better protect their sensitive data and assets in the dynamic and evolving landscape of cloud computing.

Conclusion

In summary, the "CCSP: Certified Cloud Security Professional - Novice to Certified" book bundle provides a comprehensive and structured approach to mastering the intricacies of cloud security. Across the four books, readers embark on a journey from foundational concepts to expert-level insights, covering all aspects essential for becoming a Certified Cloud Security Professional (CCSP).

In "Foundations of Cloud Security: A Beginner's Guide to CCSP," readers are introduced to the fundamental principles and components of cloud security, laying the groundwork for understanding more advanced topics. This book equips novices with the necessary knowledge and skills to navigate the complexities of cloud security confidently.

"Securing Cloud Infrastructure: Advanced Techniques for CCSP" delves into advanced techniques and strategies for securing cloud infrastructure effectively. From securing multi-cloud environments to implementing advanced encryption and access controls, this book empowers readers with the expertise needed to tackle complex security challenges in modern cloud environments.

"Risk Management in the Cloud: Strategies for CCSP Professionals" provides a comprehensive exploration of risk management principles and strategies tailored specifically for cloud environments. Readers learn how to identify, assess, and mitigate risks effectively, ensuring the security and resilience of cloud-based systems and applications.

Finally, "Mastering Cloud Security: Expert Insights and Best Practices for CCSP Certification" offers expert insights and best practices from seasoned professionals in the field. This book goes beyond theoretical concepts to provide practical guidance and real-world examples, enabling readers to apply their knowledge effectively and achieve CCSP certification with confidence.

Together, these four books form a comprehensive and cohesive resource that empowers readers to become proficient in cloud security and excel in their careers as Certified Cloud Security Professionals. Whether you are just starting your journey in cloud security or seeking to enhance your expertise, this book bundle equips you with the knowledge, skills, and confidence needed to succeed in today's dynamic and ever-evolving cloud landscape.

www.ingramcontent.com/pod-product-compliance
Lightning Source LLC
Chambersburg PA
CBHW071233050326
40690CB00011B/2101